S0-CTA-841

Four-Foot Cucumbers, Juvenile Delinquents
&
Frogs from the Sky!

"YOU'LL NEVER MISS THE WATER"

Four-Foot Cucumbers, Juvenile Delinquents
&
Frogs from the Sky!

Snippets of Life in Victorian Canada

Crystal Fulton
&
Glen C. Phillips

Cheshire Cat Press
London, Canada

CHESHIRE CAT PRESS
1110-95 Fiddler's Green Road
London, Ontario, Canada   N6H 4T1
(519) 472-5572

© Crystal Fulton and Glen C. Phillips, 1997
All rights reserved.

Printed in Canada by
Aylmer Express Limited
Aylmer, Ontario

10 9 8 7 6 5 4 3 2 1

Canadian Cataloguing in Publication Data

Fulton, Crystal, 1965-
   Four-foot cucumbers, juvenile delinquents & frogs from the sky!:
snippets of life in Victorian Canada

ISBN 0-921818-18-1

1. Canada - Social life and customs - 19th century.* 2. Canada -
Social life and customs - 19th century - Sources.* 3. Canadian
newspapers - Social aspects. I. Phillips, Glen C. II. Title.

FC88.F85 1997   971   C97-932478-5
F1021.F85 1997

This book was gratefully researched, written, and published
without the aid of any kind of public grant whatsoever.

Contents

Preface

A few years ago, while sifting through some back issues of the *Sarnia Observer*, Glen fell upon the idea for this book. The idea, however, lay dormant for quite some time, until Crystal's enthusiasm for it rekindled Glen's. Fueled by great curiosity, we then trekked through several miles of microfilm in search of insightful press commentary about Canadian life a century ago. From the resulting tower of about 2,000 transcribed newspaper passages, we next selected the snippets that appear in the following pages. It was a wonderful journey of discovery, and we feel richer for the experience.

Of course, this work is not the result of our energies alone. We would like to thank the librarians who went beyond the call of duty to assist us. We especially tip our hats to the staffs at the D.B. Weldon Library, U.W.O., and at the National Library of Canada. We would also like to acknowledge the warm accommodations that Sandra Hollingshead and Scott and Jean Jordan shared with us while we were in Ottawa. In addition, we would like to thank the dozens of newspaper publishers and editors who permitted us to quote freely from the historical columns of their journals.

Finally, the ultimate purpose of this book is to provide readers with a novel view of Victorian Canada. Rather than spinning out endless heaps of dry interpretation, we want to give Canadians an accessible and entertaining treatment of the past that allows the voice of our predecessors to be heard. Above all, we truly hope that those who delve into these pages will get as much enjoyment out of this book as we did putting it together.

Crystal Fulton & Glen C. Phillips
London, Ontario, Canada
October, 1997

Introduction

At its very essence, this book is a selected collection of nearly 600 passages gleaned from the "local" columns of over 250 English-language newspapers published in Canada during the period 1867 to 1900. Newspapers are not only a means of communication, but a fascinating record of culture. Historically speaking, they are an amazing window through which we can peer to discover our past. Victorian journals reveal that our forebears, as insightful or as unremarkable as it may sound, share with us much the same concerns, interests, and life experiences. If readers find this somewhat hard to swallow, they should first compare what they encounter in these pages with any newscast televised in this country today. Despite a vain presumption that we live in the most advanced and progressive era the globe has ever witnessed, we have yet to move beyond the Victorians' fondness for feeding off the misery and anguish of others or delighting in news about freaks of nature, even if our "freak shows" are dressed up as TV talk shows and the tabloid media. Indeed, in many respects, we have not really changed that much.

The press excerpts included in this work all meet one simple criterion - they illuminate what life, however typical or extraordinary, was like in nineteenth-century Canada. The passages have been organized thematically by chapter, and with few exceptions, they appear chronologically within each chapter. In turn, a contextual preamble introduces each chapter. Despite this book's arrangement, readers are sure to notice a handful of common strands that thread the topics together. For instance, while Victorian Canadians frequently exhibited a strong belief in order and an upright degree of formality, they also displayed a keen sense of playfulness.

For the most part, the newspaper snippets appear as they were originally published. However, obvious grammatical and typographical errors have been corrected. Square brackets denote words or phrases that have been added to improve our understanding of colloquial phrases and implied meanings. And although Victorian syntax has been generally preserved, awkward sentences have been rearranged for the reader's benefit. Finally, our predecessors did not seem to be too concerned with what we now deem Canadian or American spellings, such as neighbour/neighbor. If anything, many newspapers disregarded the "u" to save time and money in the compositing room and to conserve space in the finished product.

In closing, a few comments are necessary about the newspapers themselves. Above all, it should be noted that every nineteenth-century journalist wrote with some sort of partiality. While their political views are usually quite obvious, their largely middle-class, Anglo-Saxon, and often protestant outlook is implicit. In this regard, this book is as much about Canada's Victorian press as it is about life in the 1800s. Ontario's dominant role looms as another bias in the national newspaper industry of a century ago. Indeed, in 1881, Ontario's astounding sum of 373 papers absolutely dwarfed Quebec's tally of 88, the country's second highest provincial total. Nonetheless, the excerpts which follow constitute a fairly balanced geographic representation of the Victorian Canadian experience. Readers will undoubtedly enjoy exploring our nation's past from the Atlantic to the Pacific and almost to the Arctic. A gazetteer of newspapers concludes this work.

Chapter One

Politics & National Issues

Since Confederation, profound diversities in the ethnic, cultural, economic, and geographic experiences of Canadians have shaped, reshaped and inevitably tested the Dominion's political landscape. Indeed, these differences gave rise to initial Maritime opposition to the federal scheme, stalled the entrance of B.C. and P.E.I. into the Canadian union, and made Louis Riel's defiance a divisive force in our past.

However, Confederation also brought people together to forge a common destiny. Faith in the young Dominion's prospects, loyalty to the British Empire and Queen Victoria, and even criticism of the United States were just some of the bonds that united our forebears. A host of other topics also tied Canadians together. Foreshadowing what we now mull over endlessly, such issues as the dishonesty of politicians, patronage, the merits of our impotent senate, government overspending, the rising cost of postage, and, of course, taxes received ample and universal consideration in printers' ink.

Above all, however, the nineteenth century was the era of the political tabloid. With few exceptions, journalists made no secret of their politics. Dedicated soldiers on both sides of a two-party system, the vast majority of Canadian newspaper writers were either Tory or Grit, and they steadfastly supported their political friends and eagerly hurled venomous barbs at their opponents. As the foremost politician of his time, Sir John A. Macdonald figured prominently in such debate. Not surprisingly, Canadians either reviled or worshipped *the* Father of Confederation.

The new Dominion of Canada was ushered in at Peter-borough by the discharge of heavy guns, muskets, etc., the ringing of bells, and various other marks of general rejoicing of the citizens. To many, the ringing of the bells was a cause for alarm, but very soon they found that their fears were groundless; the cause was nothing more than introducing our citizens to Confederation.

Peterborough Examiner, July 4, 1867

It is rumored that the Government intends shortly to pardon five of the Fenian convicts now in the Provincial Penitentiary, as an act of clemency to mark the inauguration of the new Dominion. It is said that the Rev. J. McMahon is to be one of the number.

Belleville Intelligencer, July 9, 1867

An extraordinary and disgraceful outrage was committed in London, Ontario last Friday night by a set of low, mongrel Grits. It being understood that Messrs. Glass and Carling would return to town on the night train, after having taken part in the Bothwell election contest, a crowd of roughs, headed by those two notorious individuals, Messrs. Cornish and Peacock, proceeded to the railway station, and when the gentlemen above named stepped off the cars, they were assailed with a tempest of yells, groans and rotten eggs, and followed through the streets by the howling faction. That Mr. Carling, who was lately elected to represent the city in both the House of Commons and Provincial Legislature by over-whelming majorities, should be thus grossly insulted by a handful of Grit rowdies, led on by their defeated leaders, is a piece of audacity that is positively astounding. On the other side of the line, such an occurrence would occasion no sur-prise, but it really seems that Clear Grit bigotry and violence surpasses even rank Republicanism. This glaring outrage is a stain upon the fair fame of London that cannot be easily wiped out, but it will tend still further to open the eyes of our people to the true nature of the defeated and disreputable faction who seeks to control the dimes and destinies of this Province.

St. Catharines Constitutional, September 26, 1867

THE DARK AGES IN CANADA - A tax on books, a tax on newspapers, a tax on coal oil.

Huntingdon Canadian Gleaner, May 8, 1868

British Columbia is now CANADA, and we admire the pluck with which the government has grasped the future requirements of what we hope to be in some future day a great empire more British than Britain.

Niagara News, April 5, 1871

BANKRUPTCY - If the Dominion Government carries out its Pacific Railway scheme it will add at least $150,000,000 to our debt, and the Dominion will be compelled to borrow $10,000,000 yearly to pay the interest and working expenses. When a private individual has to borrow money to pay the interest on his debts he is declared bankrupt. Nova Scotia will have to bear a portion of the heavy burden and share in the general humiliation. Confederation is responsible for all this, and therefore, Nova Scotians should again condemn that scheme at the polls.

New Glasgow Eastern Chronicle, April 27, 1871

All loyal hearts will rejoice to hear that Her Majesty Queen Victoria has fully recovered from her recent illness.

Newcastle Union Advocate, September 14, 1871

Newfoundland still holds out against Confederation. The recent elections in that island have again resulted in the defeat of the Union Party. St. John's has elected six members

11

all opposed to the "policy of the Crown." In many parts of the island there was no opposition to the Anti-Confederate candidates.

Yarmouth Herald, November 23, 1871

Love-letter ink, so called because it disappears in about four weeks' time, is the latest thing out in the writing fluid line. It is not only a favorite with inconsistent lovers for letters, but is being adopted by parties doing business with I.O.U.'s and by politicians in drafting their political opinions.

St. Catharines Weekly News, November 14, 1872

It is the intention of the Government to withdraw, as soon as possible, the circulation of the 20 cent silver piece, which on account of its similarity to the 25 cent piece is considered a public nuisance.

Ormstown New Dominion, May 14, 1874

Louis Riel, having been formally outlawed, cannot claim the seat for Provencher in the House of Commons to which he was recently re-elected.

Renfrew Mercury, October 23, 1874

Today the free system of postal delivery will be commenced. It will no doubt be welcomed by citizens generally. The carriers will appear in uniform in due course of time. There will be three deliveries each day. Notice giving full instructions in regard thereto have been published for the information of the public.

Ottawa Times, May 1, 1875

The London Free Press (Tory) says "the country is going to the devil." The Toronto Mail (Tory) says "the country is going to Sir John A. Macdonald." Six of one and half a dozen of the other.

Ingersoll Chronicle [Grit], April 11, 1878

A Sweet Trio - Sir John A. Macdonald, leader of the Tory opposition, MacDougall of Three Rivers, and C.J. Campbell were all beastly drunk in the House of Commons at Ottawa on Saturday night last. This is an undeniable fact.

Ingersoll Chronicle, April 18, 1878

The color line has extended into Canada. Two citizens of Toronto were refused admittance to the skating rink because of their color.

Montreal Star, January 20, 1882

"Onderdonkey" is a new word coined by the London [Ontario] Advertiser to describe Sir Charles Tupper's system of giving contracts to the highest instead of the lowest tenderer. It is a good word - a very good word.

Pontiac News, April 27, 1882

This is Dominion Day and there is no celebration programme. The Canadian element in our community is not very strong. We have hunted up the best maple leaf we could find and will wear it as an emblem of the land of our nationality. By and by, as Calgary grows, Dominion Day will doubtless be the day par excellence as it is in the eastern provinces.

Calgary Nor'wester, July 1, 1884

The H.M.S. Tenedos went northward on a fishery protection cruise yesterday morning.

St. John's Newfoundlander, September 12, 1884

The friendship which has always existed along the border, between the inhabitants of Uncle Sam's dominions and those of our beloved Queen, was broken asunder on Saturday last, when a large crowd of the Yanks, armed with sticks and chunks of ice, tried to drive the Canucks off the ice in the St.

Clair River. The Canucks, seeing they were outnumbered, though not outgeneraled, came to their native soil, and getting reinforcements, proceeded to the scene of battle, where they routed the enemy, and took possession of the field. The boys deserve a chromo for their bravery in routing the enemy.

Sarnia Observer, February 6, 1885

It is a sorry sight to see the death sentence passed on Louis Riel respited from time to time merely to allow Cabinet Ministers to wrangle over what should be done in the matter. After all, it is little wonder that they prolong the day of causing a man to be hanged for the crimes he committed through their neglect and blundering. Monday next has been appointed by Sir John for the fatal bolt to spring.

Prescott Telegraph, November 13, 1885

The Riel has found its rope.

Qu'Appelle Progress, November 20, 1885

Mr. Nat Moore's parrot caught the election fever and now shrieks out, "Hurrah for Bergin [local M.P.]" with surprisingly distinct tones.

Cornwall Standard, March 3, 1887

Fred Mowat, son of the Hon. Oliver Mowat [Liberal], has been appointed Sheriff of Toronto. It is one of the fattest offices in Ontario. What a howl there would have been in the Liberal camp had a son of Sir John A. Macdonald received such an office, the gift of the Dominion Premier. Now let the Grits shut up forever.

Brampton Conservator, May 6, 1887

Senator McInnes has introduced a bill to make Gaelic an official language in Canada.

Moose Jaw Times, February, 28, 1890

14

The Toronto Telegram says that the World's Fair in Chicago has been a financial failure, but it has served the good purpose of reducing the swelled heads of Yankees who believed that all Christendom would prostrate itself before the shrine of American genius.

Parkhill Gazette-Review, September 28, 1893

The poor old Canadian Senate! Principal Grant [of Queen's Univ.] says, "We have succeeded in getting the most useless Second Chamber in the world. The great objection to our senate is that it is simply an addition to the bribery fund at the disposal of the Premier." The Principal is exactly right.

Port Elgin Times, November 15, 1893

A milking machine, which is said to milk 10 cows at a time, is being treated with a view to being used in this province. We cannot help thinking that some device of the kind has been at work in Ottawa for some time past. The systematic and general way in which railway subsidies and other government expenditures have been made to yield their richness to Tory campaign funds makes is difficult to believe that the milking was done by hand.

Lanark Era, August 21, 1895

"A change!" is the cry all over the Dominion. Tupperism is doomed. Mr. Laurier will be premier on the evening of June 23rd. Vote for Dr. McLennan, the Liberal candidate.

Port Hawkesbury Bulletin, June 19, 1896

Canadian postage on first class matter is too high.

Cardston Record, September 10, 1898

Chapter Two

Matters Municipal

While provincial and federal governments were charged with such supreme duties as creating law, shaping public policy, and developing overarching economic strategies, the municipal level of civic administration played the most prominent role in Canadians' lives during the nineteenth century. Quite simply, municipal councils dealt with the day-to-day problems that faced the populace. Moreover, the actions of local government were more tangible. Tariffs and statutes were important enough, but municipal improvements, such as sidewalks, sewers, water supply, street numbering, and the regulation of daily nuisances, such as dusty thoroughfares, errant bovines, and free-roaming dogs, were, if newspaper columns are any indication, of greater consequence to people's daily experience.

On this score, the Victorian press assumed the role of civic watchdog. Acting on their subscribers' behalf, journalists, in an unrelenting torrent of words, reminded councillors about their duty to stay on top of municipal issues. Aside from keeping councils abreast of local concerns, newspapers also conveyed ratepayers' impatience with the tardy, irregular, or even nonexistent delivery of municipal services. While often veiled in humour, rebuke in this regard was often quite biting and ran quickly to the point. And like today, members of the public routinely reserved slim tolerance for the oversights of their municipal leaders.

Our Sidewalks - Schomberg has the name, far and wide, of being a prosperous, go-ahead little village, but if some of our go-ahead folks don't tumble down and break their necks before long, it won't be because there are not traps enough in the sidewalks. Who will move in the matter?

Schomberg Standard, September 13, 1867

Look to the Sewers! - Several of the sewers, owing, we presume to the unusual dryness and warmth of the season, are beginning already to give off offensive odours. We hope the Sanitary Committee will look after this matter in time.

Victoria British Columbian, March 23, 1869

Accident - We regret to learn that while Mr. Jared Irwin, Jr., of Yonge Street, was crossing over the Bradford bridge on Monday last, his horse took fright and kicked him on the leg so seriously as to necessitate amputation below the knee. The operation was performed by Dr. Morton, of Bradford, assisted by Dr. Hackett, of Newmarket. From last accounts, Mr. Irwin was doing as well as could be expected.

Newmarket Era, June 17, 1870

Heavy Suit - Mr. Jared Irwin, Jr., of Yonge Street near Newmarket, who got his leg broken last spring by a kick from his horse, which was frightened by the dangerous state of the road within the limits of Bradford, near the bridge over the Holland River, has brought an action against the Corporation of that place for $10,000 in damages. His leg had to be amputated to save his life.

Newmarket Era, January 13, 1871

What is the use of street lamps when they are lighted only after nine o'clock in the evening? If the lamplighter has no time to light them all at the proper hour, he should commence at five o'clock in the morning.

Sorel Pilot, August 9, 1877

The eye of ye Thames Street merchant glistened with joy yesterday afternoon at the sight of the watering cart. The dust of the past two weeks has done an immense amount of damage to goods.

Ingersoll Chronicle, April 18, 1878

Why is it that cattle are allowed to run at large on Sunday? Is it to destroy peoples' gardens, or is it that the taxes are so light that the police are not paid for Sunday?

Prince Edward Island Farmer, August 21, 1878

Stratford town council have decided to prohibit cows from running at large inside the corporation. If our town council enforced a law of that kind, the fun of dodging around the cow-slips that cover the sidewalks would be utterly spoiled.

Sarnia Observer, April 29, 1879

The following letter endorsed "Remorse" and signed by "Cow-catcher" was received by Chief Constable Windred the other day, along with a cow-bell: "I herewith forward to you a cow-bell and strap captured from a cow violating the cow by-law at 12 o'clock last night. The slumbers of the peaceful on Dufferin Avenue and Lorne Square are constantly broken by said cow and the 'tin-tinnabulations of the bell;' and we forward the same to you in grateful recognition of your services in carrying out the provisions of the cow by-law. Hoping you will have a *bully* time wearing the same, I remain, &c."

Sarnia Observer, August 12, 1881

The drinking fountain erected on the corner of Talbot and Dundas Streets for the "convenience" of the public is very thoughtfully provided with tin cups, both of which lack bottoms.

London Advertiser, October 12, 1882

We understand that it is Ald. Davis' intention to introduce a by-law at the next meeting of the City Council with a view of having all the houses in town *numbered*. The cost would not be felt, and the advantages would be very great. This is an idea that this paper has advocated from time to time, and we trust that it will command the unanimous support of the Mayor and City Council.

Fredericton Evening Capital, April 22, 1884

The fish market nuisance has again commenced on Market Square. Cannot something be done to provide a more suitable site, and thereby give wholesome air around the present quarter?

Charlottetown Daily Examiner, May 13, 1886

That carcass of a horse to the north of the town should be buried before warm weather sets in. The vicinity has been the rendevous for dogs of all sizes, shapes, ages and breeds, and, humanlike, they have their family jars.

Fort William Journal, April 14, 1887

The water-carriers have been notified that they must take their supply from above the town, owing to a number of drains and sewers that empty into the river above the point where they have been taking their supply from.

Fort William Journal, April 21, 1887

People are complaining every day about the racket made at night by a lot of useless curs that are allowed to run around town. The constable has no place to put impounded canines; therefore, the blame falls on the shoulders of our civic fathers.

Prince Albert Times, August 3, 1888

The dog nuisance grows apace. At the last meeting of the London Township Council, $212.49 was voted to owners of sheep that had been killed or mangled by dogs, besides the $13 voted to the valuator - total $225.49. There is nothing to show that the proprietors of the sheep-mangling curs pay a cent of dog tax. The moral is obvious.

London Advertiser, July 12, 1889

There is something wrong with the inlet pipe of the water works. Minnows and young herring, all alive, have been discharged from the water pipes in various parts of the town during the past week. The sensation created by finding these wrigglers in one's drinking water, especially in the dark, is not a pleasant one, even though they may be taken as a guarantee of the purity of the water.

Sarnia Observer, March 28, 1890

Once more we direct the attention of the authorities to the disgraceful condition of our cemetery. Cattle trample over the newly made graves, pallings are broken and the whole place presents a sickening appearance.

Regina Standard, June 19, 1891

Wellington Street was the scene of a horse race last evening. this dangerous practice of running horses on public streets in town where the lives of pedestrians are at their mercy from being run over, ought to be stopped. It seems that there is no such law governing such practices and it is time the Council should enact by-laws to cover this ground.

Chilliwack Progress, July 2, 1891

What this city requires is a thorough reconstruction of the water works system - not an attempt to cover up the facts regarding the quality of the water now being supplied.

Toronto Evening News, April 8, 1893

Chapter Three

Flora & Fauna

Victorian Canadians lived much closer to the natural world than we do today. In the first place, well over half the population lived on farms where animals were not only raised as livestock, but also employed as motive power. Moreover, farm families gained firsthand experience with the varieties of crops and weeds that sprouted in their fields, as well as with the pests that scurried and flew about their farmsteads. Urbanites were also intimately familiar with plants and animals. Townsfolk, too, used literal horsepower, and they often kept vegetable, herb, and flower gardens, and raised cows and hens for a daily supply of fresh milk and eggs. Of course, many had dogs for companionship and household security in a world of very dark nights. In addition, cats were not only pets, but also on-the-spot pest exterminators.

It should, therefore, come as little surprise that our predecessors rendered broad commentary about the living environment that surrounded them. Through the newspaper, they shared reports about everything from the overabundance of wandering dogs to human interaction with wild animals, including the ravenous *mosquitoeus Canadensis*. Since they viewed the living world as a well-ordered system, which fell under their prerogative to dominate, Victorian Canadians expressed their greatest wonder at those natural oddities, such as mammoth radishes, boss potatoes, four-foot cucumbers, educated pigs, two-headed calves, and wintertime butterflies, which reminded them that nature was indeed more powerful than they and truly under the stewardship of a higher power.

A Disorderly Dog - About nine o'clock yesterday morning, a dog jumped through a large light [pane] of glass in the door of Mr. Charles McNab's dry goods establishment, corner of John and King Streets.

Hamilton Spectator, February 7, 1867

Dogs are mysteriously disappearing in Ottawa just now. Probably the influx of so many Parliamentarians into that city may have increased the demand for sausage meat.

Sackville Borderer, April 3, 1868

One day last week, as Mr. Joseph Lapp was making some repairs in his house, while pulling down the chimney in the garret, between the chimney and the siding one of his men found part of a $5 bill, which the mice had carried there and destroyed. Unfortunately the serial number was gone.

Markham Economist, August 26, 1869

Lusus Nature - Mr. J.E. Harrison, Veterinary Surgeon, informs us of a curious freak of nature that came under his professional notice. A cow belonging to Mr. David Kenny, 6th line, Trafalgar Township, last Monday gave birth to a calf having two complete and well-formed heads. The calf was born alive, but died shortly afterwards.

Milton Canadian Champion, May 12, 1870

THE CHAMPION TAPE WORM - A man in Widder Village, named Collinge, last week passed a tape worm over thirty feet long. This sounds tough to believe, but is really the case, as the worm may be seen by the unbelieving at any time in the surgery of Dr. Bice, who attended the man in his sickness.

London Free Press, July 18, 1870

Mammoth Radish - Mr. William S. Kenney, proprietor of the

"Central House" hotel, Barrington, has sent us a radish raised in his garden weighing 31 pounds and 1 ounce.

Yarmouth Herald, November 30, 1871

Mr. Douglas Chase, Lower Mangerville, Sunbury, has a hog one year and six months old that stands three feet, eight inches high, and girts six feet, two inches. He is nine feet in length. Mr. Chase expects that, by next fall, this hog will weigh one thousand pounds. Considerable of a hog certainly. Where in the Dominion can his equal be found?

Fredericton Colonial Farmer, January 22, 1872

Dogs and Sheep - Mr. Rainsford, whose sheep have lately been decimated by a dog, determined to watch the canine last Friday, and did so all day, but having gone into the bushes for a few minutes to drag out the carcass of a sheep that had been killed the day before, he found on his return that the dog had been watching him and had, in his absence, killed seven of his sheep. A smart dog; too smart to be at large.

Fredericton Colonial Farmer, June 3, 1872

The Compton Ghost - We have reliable information that "the ghost" that is said to have frightened so many of the evening promenaders near the village of Compton Centre is nothing more than a "corn crake," a small bird that makes a peculiar noise with its bill. Our informant was within 20 feet of it, and says he could have caught it had the ground not been swampy.

Sherbrooke Gazette, August 9, 1872

Boss Potato - Mr. John James of the second concession of Drummond has handed us what for size and appearance is one of the most extraordinary potatoes we have ever seen. It consists of a main or daddy potato with five smaller of children potatoes attached. It was grown upon Mr. James' farm, weighs two pounds and a quarter, and may be seen in the Expositor window. Bring on your Murphies. Where's John Weston this year? Perth Expositor.

Kingston Daily News, September 26, 1873

Mr. Arthur Davison is the champion carrot grower of the town, so far as our knowledge goes, and this is derived from the fact that he has sent us a lot of fine Early Horn and Long Orange varieties, some of which are 18 inches long and show excellent cultivation.

Amherst Gazette, October 24, 1873

Rats - A gentleman residing on the Richmond Road has just rid his premises of rats in a very expeditious manner. It appears that the little rodent animals infested his premises in immense numbers, destroying everything before them. Finally, he procured a weasel, which he fed for a while by giving it live rats, which it killed and devoured. He then let the weasel go and in a few days afterwards there was not a rat to be seen about the place.

Ottawa Free Press, July 15, 1874

In some sections of this neighborhood, the grasshoppers have been very destructive, pastures being eaten bare and oats and spring wheat being much injured. The only remedy against these pests is a good drove of turkeys, which will soon sweep a field of them.

Clinton New Era, July 30, 1874

Mr. John McKay, a farmer in the Township of Dunwich, a little north of Dutton, has caught a living snake with two heads on one body. The heads are not joined together and are perfectly formed, with two eyes in each head. This wonderful snake will eat and drink with each head, and sometimes with both heads at once. Can P.T. Barnum beat this?

Embro Planet, September 9, 1874

A Wonderful Fish - An immense mackerel, measuring nine feet in length and weighing over five hundred pounds, was caught off Devil's Island on last Friday evening.

Digby Weekly Courier, October 16, 1874

Jack, the dog that watches the Collingwood post office, is a wise dog in his way. The other day a gentleman went out of the office and forgot his gloves, whereupon Jack picked the gloves up in his mouth, tracked the gentleman until he found him, and very politely presented the gloves.

Clinton New Era, February 4, 1875

Dundas is now overrun with goats, greatly to the annoyance of many citizens who do not care to be unceremoniously "butted" at every street corner.

Clinton New Era, April 15, 1875

Butter is rather a scarce article in Granby nowadays. Some say the cows have struck for higher prices; others say that they are devoting their time to rearing young bovines.

Granby Gazette, May 7, 1875

Boss Cucumber - Mr. Althouse of Strathroy has presented us with a cucumber four feet long. As he has some left that are even longer than the above, the gentry of Watford should import a car load and wear them on the left side of the coat as roses have disappeared.

Watford Advocate, August 27, 1875

A snake of the class known as blue racers, measuring upwards of ten feet in length, and eight or ten inches around, has been seen at Aylmer.

Woodstock Weekly Review, August 27, 1875

Mammoth Corn - A West Zorra Township gentleman, whose name it is not necessary to mention here, cultivated a few hills of Rabourdine Corn this season, the mammoth proportions of which are astonishing. It stands nearly fifteen feet high, and the stalk measures five inches in circumference, while some of the leaves are ten inches in width. It is certainly the biggest corn ever seen in this township, and we challenge Ontario to produce a larger specimen of any variety. Woodstock Planet.

Woodstock Weekly Review, August 27, 1875

A Large Halibut - On Friday last, Mr. Henry Massey and Mr. Edward Mosher were out fishing near Ironbound Shoals off Kingsburg, Lunenburg County, when they captured an immense halibut, which to kill they had to weigh their anchor and use the grapplin as a club. The fish measured 12 feet, 9 inches in length and six feet in width, and made two and a half barrels [worth of fillets].

Halifax Citizen, October 20, 1875

Mammoth Ox - We saw Messrs. Etter, Buckley & Company's big ox weighed yesterday. His weight is 2,720 pounds, girth 9 feet. He is six years old, was raised by Mr. George Etter, Westmoreland, and is probably the largest in the Dominion.

Amherst Gazette, April 14, 1876

Two men exhibited a gentle, harmless, little muzzled bear through the streets of the town last Saturday. The wee bit of an animal, which is about the size of an ordinary elephant, performed some gentle little tricks to the delight and amuse-ment of a large crowd of children and full grown people.

Sorel Pilot, June 14, 1877

Two of Mr. McClafferty's children from Tannery Street were interviewed by a bear cub a few days ago while the youngsters were berrying on the Mountain Road in the rear of the Jones' land. Young Bruin ate blueberries out of the children's hands, and otherwise conducted himself after the manner of his race.

Moncton Daily Times, August 21, 1877

On the 5th of February '78, a yellow butterfly flew into the house of Mr. Nelson of Scott. It was caught and placed in a box, and brought to us yesterday evening. It is still lively and apparently quite comfortable.

Uxbridge Journal, February 7, 1878

A cow belonging to Mr. J. Gould of Seymour East gave birth last week to a natural phenomenon in the shape of twins, the singular creatures being connected at the hips and having two heads, two tails, and seven legs. Both died, however, soon afterwards.

Orangeville Sun, April 25, 1878

Buffalo continue to advance on this settlement, and are now quite numerous fifty miles south. Several parties of hunters have gone from town to secure a supply of meat for their use this winter.

Saskatchewan Herald, September 23, 1878

The wolves recently killed a colt belonging to the Macfarlane Brothers, and on the next night a very large wolf, which returned to finish up the feast, partook of a little poison and died on the spot. It measured seven feet, six inches from the nose to the tip of the tail.

Saskatchewan Herald, December 30, 1878

There was on exhibition on Saturday in the window of Mr. A.C. Smith's store, Market Building, a turnip weighing 23 pounds. It came from Mr. T. Bradley's farm, Mace's Bay, Charlotte County.

St. John Daily News, December 1, 1879

A large sturgeon about 12 feet long was on show at Herring's "Original" store on Front Street. It yielded about a barrel of fine caviar.

New Westminster Mainland Guardian, March 13, 1880

Struck a Whale - The schooner Oriole, Captain A. Mayer, on the 16th ultimo, while on the way to Bute Inlet, and near Horny Island, ran slap bang into a whale. His whaleship received a rude awakening from his mid-day siesta, and the schooner was almost brought to a stand-still, the bow rising several feet in the air. Nothing hurt. Nanaimo Free Press.

Kamloops Inland Sentinel, July 8, 1880

The season of big eggs has now arrived. Our exchanges are trotting out their prodigies in that line. The Gleaner has one 14 ½ inches the long way and 1 1/4 pounds in weight.

Beaverton Express, April 15, 1882

A new danger has arisen to annoy the unprotected female. And it touches a very tender spot, too - the headgear. A Miss Singleton of Riverside wore a very charming bonnet with "such lovely flowers, you know." Well, the bees got on to those artificial flowers, taking them for the genuine article, and perhaps out of revenge for their disappointment, stung the young lady severely about the face and neck.

Collingwood Enterprise, July 27, 1882

A few nights ago an insignificant mink found its way into a hen-roost belonging to the Rev. Mr. Roddick of Brandon Hills, and in the morning, in throwing open the door, the rev. found that fifty-two hens had perished by the foul attack. The entire flock in the space of a few hours was swept off. A number of other settlers have suffered in the same way.

Brandon Mail, April 10, 1883

That beautiful, streaked-back, odoriferous little creature, the "Mephitis Americana," or more commonly called skunk, is now abroad.

Campbellford Herald, April 26, 1883

Mystic News - There are some large insects in Farnham woods, if all stories are true. A man who went to peel bark, taking his dinner with him, reports that while he was away from his work in search of water, a huge mosquito ate his dinner and used his bark spud for a toothpick.

Missisquoi Record, June 5, 1885

A calf with two faces on one head is on exhibition in Pictou. The manager of the curiosity is a blind man named Nelson of St. Mary's, Nova Scotia.

Charlottetown Daily Examiner, May 29, 1886

Bears are on the rampage in the vicinity of Little Current and are after the livestock.

Fort William Journal, May 19, 1887

A young turkey hatched in J. Price's flock this spring had four legs and two tails on one body. It did not seem likely to thrive and Mr. Price killed it.

Edmonton Bulletin, June 18, 1887

The cow which Mr. R.P. Perry lost a few days ago was found in a well.

Muskoka Herald, June 21, 1888

A fine cougar in excellent condition and measuring about 7 feet, 6 inches was shot by W. McGeer, dairyman, on his premises early yesterday morning. The blood-thirsty animal had been after his sheep, so Mr. McGeer laid in wait for him and polished him off as soon as he came within easy range.

Vancouver Weekly World, September 5, 1889

James McGeer is bewailing the demise of his six-legged colt.
Vancouver Weekly World, September 5, 1889

Station Agent Fowler's piscatorial enterprise is not proving a success. About a week ago both his gold fish expired from a chilling of the water, and this week he mourns the loss of a gold-eye which committed suicide by leaping out of the aquarium onto the floor.
Medicine Hat Times, January 30, 1890

Neepawa will celebrate the 24th of May by a monster gopher hunt in which all the neighboring municipalities will take part.
Moose Jaw Times, May 9, 1890

Inwood News - The tape worm doctor visited our town on Tuesday and showed the finest collection of that specimen we ever saw. The longest was 175 feet without a break.
Petrolia Topic, November 14, 1890

The other day a curiosity was exhibited at Wingham in the shape of a large wasp's nest. The nest was found by James McConnell of Hullett Township and measures 5 feet in circumference. It is peculiarly shaped, almost round, and built on a branch an inch in diameter, which runs directly through the centre of the nest.
Aylmer Express, December 19, 1890

Master Henry Murphy brought in to us a bunch of full-blown pansies on Tuesday, picked in the open garden the day before. Can this be equalled in Nova Scotia?
Wolfville Acadian & Berwick Times, January 30, 1891

In clearing away the debris prior to erecting a new dwelling house for Mr. D. O'Leary, the workmen discovered a live hen imprisoned beneath one of the walls, 8 days after the fire. Her henship was apparently none the worse after her prolonged fast.

Richibucto Review, February 12, 1891

Two dogs of this town have formed themselves into a society for the destruction of grouse, prairie chickens, and other birds now hatching. They should be tied up.

Vernon News, June 18, 1891

The largest and handsomest salmon of the season has just been caught in the Fraser River. It weighed 45 pounds and was three and a half feet long. It has been sent to Ottawa as a present to the Hon. E. Dewdney, Minister of the Interior, by Mr. W.H. Vinan of New Westminster in memory of old times on the Fraser.

Chilliwack Progress, June 18, 1891

Arthur Hibbert, a little lad about 6 years old who resides with his parents on the old Dobson place, was bitten by a rattle-snake Friday night as he came out of the chicken coup. Dr. Pare was sent for and he succeeded in saving the little fellow's life. The rattler was found and killed. He had nine rattles. His mate was also killed. The place abounds with rattle-snakes.

Windsor Evening Record, July 5, 1893

Mosquitoes, black flies, sand flies, and deer flies are doing a roaring business among the cattle in Algoma. The poor brutes groan with pain. It is a great blessing that the fly season there is a short one.

Alliston Weekly Herald, July 9, 1893

A cherry tree in the garden of Mr. Walter A. Brant of the Indian Reserve is in full bloom for the second time this year.

Deseronto Tribune, October 6, 1893

William Warnock of Goderich exhibits at the World's Fair a milk-white squash, which weighs 486 pounds and measures over 11 feet in circumference.

Deseronto Tribune, October 20, 1893

Sylvan News - An apple grown this year in the orchard of Mr. William Randall, our esteemed mail-carrier, measured 14 3/4 inches in circumference. This is 1/4 of an inch less than the apple from British Columbia which took first prize at the World's Fair.

Parkhill Gazette-Review, October 26, 1893

Provincial News - A 12 foot shark was captured last week by two boys at Coal Harbour near Vancouver. The shark was jammed between some logs.

Nelson Miner, June 9, 1894

While cutting cordwood the other day, Mr. John Bond, in splitting a cut of a big fir tree sixty feet from the root, exposed to view an Enfield rifle bullet and the track that it has made in the wood. It must have been fired a long time ago, as the place where the bullet entered was overgrown by a couple of inches of new timber.

Surrey Times, April 19, 1895

If the Buckingham frogs don't keep quiet, they'll be accused of counterfeiting. They're issuing too many "bank notes" these balmy evenings.

Buckingham Post, May 16, 1895

John Campbell, commonly known as Highland John, was attacked by a hog at James Earle's on Wednesday last, and received 2 deep gashes in the thigh. Mr. Earle says the pig is educated and takes care of the premises in his absence.

Brandon Mail, February 6, 1896

More than 40,000,000 humming birds, sun birds, orioles, gulls, seabirds, wax-wings, birds of paradise, and fly-catchers are annually used in decorating women's hats.

Berlin Daily Telegraph, January 11, 1898

A pig was born near Ridgetown the other day with four ears, eight legs, and four hams. This is the kind packing house men have been waiting for.

Tilbury Times, June 10, 1898

The Northwest government has issued a pamphlet on noxious weeds, the information regarding which has been supplied by James Fletcher, botanist to the Dominion experimental farms. Cuts are given of a number of the more dangerous weeds, such as tumbling mustard, ball mustard, stink weed, pepper grass, cow cockle, Russian thistle, and sweet grass, which is allied to couch grass but is more difficult to get rid of. Weeds are amongst the greatest enemies of the western farmer and the Northwest government is to be congratulated on having taken active measures to post the farmers regarding the appearance of their enemies, as well as regarding ways and means of destroying them.

Edmonton Bulletin, July 25, 1898

There are too many dogs in Sarnia: yellow dogs, brown dogs, white dogs, black dogs, spotted dogs, striped dogs, dry dogs, wet dogs, big dogs, little dogs, fat dogs, thin dogs, overfed dogs, hungry dogs, lively dogs, lazy dogs, three-legged dogs, long-tailed dogs, dogs without any tail worth speaking of, dogs with short tails, sad-eyed dogs, long-eared dogs, short-eared dogs, and dogs with one ear lacking, dogs that bark, and dogs that bite, hot dogs, cold dogs, hairy dogs, dogs that go away when you call them, and dogs that don't, cheap dogs, expensive dogs, mangy dogs, and dogs of low degree; in fact dogs of all kinds, colors, sizes, ages, and breed; too many altogether, and it would be a good thing if the worst of them were summarily made away with. Perhaps you may have some doubts regarding this statement. If so, just ask Health Officer Jehu Davis, and if his opinion does not coincide with the above, we will take it all back - every word of it.

Sarnia Observer, June 21, 1899

A landing waiter at the dock in Kingston opened an innocent-looking grip to examine it. Then he ran away as 40 rattlesnakes shoved their heads at him. The grip and contents belonged to a snake charmer.

Merrickville Star, June 29, 1899

The Edmonton Advertiser says that the report that Wednesday's north train was held up by mosquitoes between Red Deer and Strathcona is repudiated as discreditable to the mosquitoes.

Calgary Herald, July 13, 1899

Barney, the pet bear of the fire department, broke his chain and took refuge under the porch of the N.A.T. & T. Company's store. For some time all efforts to dislodge him or coax him out were in vain. He has grown lusty and strong enough to resent any undue familiarity from strangers in a way to be remembered, as several people have found out. A big lump of sugar in the hands of his friend Chief Stewart proved too much for him, however, and the hated chain was soon about his neck.

Dawson Daily News, September 12, 1899

Chapter Four

The Winter

As every Canadian knows, winter is the dominant natural feature of life in this country. To the effects of this season, we owe our favourite sport, grandparents hibernating in Florida, ritual fender-benders in November, impromptu holidays during February snowstorms, maple syrup, snowball fights, skinless tongues, frostbite, broken bones, and, of course, more ways to describe the cold than, perhaps, any other people on the globe. Moreover, our frozen season has forever made liars out of those calendars which falsely claim that winter only lasts from December to March. Just as we still do, nineteenth-century Canadians usually contended with Jack Frost from around late October until April or May. However, it was without the benefit of snow-blowers and bags of rock salt that they faced the hardships of clearing imposing barricades of snow, the dangers of ice above the head and below the feet, and the occasional cold blast from Ottawa. On the other hand, Canadians of the last century also knew the joys that winter could bring. After all, the season hardened muddy roads and permitted the leisurely indulgences of skating, tobogganning, and sleighing.

The greatest street commissioner of the age - Jack Frost, Esquire - has visited New Glasgow and our streets are now quite solid and dry, and in addition are being handsomely carpeted with snow!

New Glasgow Eastern Chronicle, December 1, 1870

St. Stephen was invaded on Monday morning by a cavalry force from Milltown under the command of Messrs. Charles H. Eaton and Charles F. Todd, who first attacked the banks (we do not mean the moneyed institutions, but the banks of snow) with an immense battering ram in the shape of a snow plough drawn by 8 horses. The assault was successful, the enemy yielding at discretion. The company declined going to Calais, Maine, Captain Eaton humorously remarking, "the taxes over there are too high." The victors then returned to Milltown and performed a similar service there, feeling that they had done nobly for their country, their altars, and their firesides. P.S. - A gentleman informs us that just 11 years ago on Monday, the late Emerson Eaton, Esquire, did similar good service with a snow plough drawn by 14 horses.

St. Croix Courier, March 28, 1872

The weather last week was so fine that we were almost induced to believe that we had seen the last of winter, but the old fellow seems to yet to be comfortably settled in the "lap of spring," for last evening the ground was quite covered with new-fallen snow.

St. John's Morning Chronicle, May 5, 1873

On Tuesday last, we are told, people in the Palmer Settlement, Jacksontown, were shovelling snow off the main high road in order to make it passable for wagons. In some places throughout the country, the snow still remains on the road to the depth of four and five feet.

Carleton Sentinel, May 8, 1875

Skating on the sidewalks is a pleasant amusement for juveniles, but doesn't add much to the comfort of pedestrians.

Watford Advocate, December 17, 1875

But few attended the market this morning and those who did had reason to regret their temerity. The wind blew like a hurricane and the intense cold penetrated to the very marrow.

Brantford Daily Expositor, December 24, 1878

March "came in like a lamb." We have had so much of the "lion" lately that we can afford to let the month go out without his company.

Saskatchewan Herald, March 10, 1879

The youngsters with their toboggans take entire possession of the sidewalks sloping towards Columbia Street and go whizzing down with the force of an avalanche. This is fine for the boys, but it may be death to some unheeding pedestrian and should be stopped. This is the second time we have had to call attention to this.

New Westminster Mainland Guardian, December 25, 1880

Wanted - a little more snow to make good sleighing.

Kemptville Advance, February 18, 1881

At the Police Court this morning the following citizens were each fined $1 for allowing snow to remain on the sidewalk in front of their premises contrary to the by-law: W.C. Clarke, Dr. Wilson, J.B. Frank, N.B. Northrup, Robert Stewart, David Serviss, and E. Corby. M.D. Ward was fined $2 and Lou Appleby's case was laid over.

Belleville Weekly Chronicle, March 17, 1882

Milder weather now. Last night the thermometer showed a temperature of 20 [Fahrenheit] below.

Brandon Mail, January 8, 1883

The safe in the banking house of Wallis, Ramsay & Co. could not be opened this morning without a six hours' struggle owing to the frost which had collected in the seams.

Brandon Mail, January 23, 1883

The cold snap emphasizes the statesmanship and goodness of heart of the Ottawa Ministers in imposing taxes upon heating fuel.

Bedford Times, February 2, 1883

While a man was walking about the west end of King Street on Tuesday, a falling icicle from the roof of the building he was passing struck him on the head, causing some injuries.

Prescott Telegraph, March 26, 1886

The rough weather on Sunday resulted in a very small attendance at the churches.

Bradford Witness, March 15, 1888

Winter has come at last and bob-sleighing and broken limbs will now be the order of the day. The doctors should certainly be thankful, as it is an ill wind that blows nobody good.

Bolton Enterprise, January 11, 1889

Trains have been very irregular during the past week owing to the severe weather all along the line. The worst point on this division seems to be Bowell Hill, where an almost continuous snow storm appears to rage. Here, the weather, though very cold, has not been stormy.

Medicine Hat Times, February 27, 1890

There was an ugly crust on the snow the greater part of last week, making it difficult for cattle to get feed, The chinook, however, came along and cleared the snow clean off.

Macleod Gazette, March 19, 1891

The cold snap again brings up for observation the peculiar exaltation and pride felt by the young man whose mustache has grown long enough to become frosted with icicles.

Hastings Star, January 25, 1893

Lumbermen report about four feet of snow in the woods.

Sudbury Journal, February 16, 1893

Two young men named Goffic and Mehan of Lebret, but who are wintering at Horse Lake, met with a very trying experience recently. They started out on the 14th instant, on horseback, accompanied by a dog, only thinly clad, to hunt up their stock, but a storm and darkness coming on they lost their bearings and were unable to reach home, and as a consequence, wandered about the prairie for 5 nights and 6 days, their only food being their dog, which they killed on their fourth day out, and about 2 ounces of bread one of them had in his pocket. They finally reached home by following the tracks of one of the search parties which went out to look for them.

Qu'Appelle Vidette, January 31, 1895

The past winter has been the mildest in the recollection of that proverbial person, "the oldest inhabitant." There has not been a genuine blizzard all winter. Some people go to Ontario to escape the cold, but got colder weather there than they would have had had they stayed home.

Wawanesa Enterprise, March 1, 1895

The worst snow storm of the year commenced last Thursday afternoon and continued until the afternoon of the next day. A strong northeast wind was blowing during the time of the storm which piled snow in big drifts, and made it most disagreeable for persons who were obliged to be out. Travelling by horse was rendered impossible and Friday's mails by stagecoach were delayed till the following day. About ten or twelve inches of snow fell. Altogether, the month of March was the stormiest and coldest month of the year and the worst March we have experienced in a long time. At present, two feet of snow cover the roads in the outlying country districts.

Antigonish Casket, April 4, 1895

Speculation is being indulged in as to what the coming winter will be like, and the weatherwise predict a severe one. They base their prophesy on two grounds - one, because September passed over without a snow storm, which indicates an early winter; the other, that fur-bearing animals are putting on a full coat of fine fur next to the skin.

Lethbridge News, October 30, 1895

It is remarked by some observers, remarks the Montreal Gazette, that the conduct and appearance of the wild animals means that this will be a cold winter. Canada's troubles are multiplying. The Grits got into parliament. Then came grasshoppers, the army worm and hog cholera. Now we are to be frozen.

Granby Mail, November 7, 1896

Toronto was brightened on Wednesday night by the first January thunderstorm in 46 years. Lightning was recorded in January 1873, and in January 1882, but it was not accompanied by thunder.

Berlin Daily Telegraph, January 14, 1898

Chapter Five

Mother Nature's Other Handiwork

Although Canada has always been known for its long, cold winters, the three other seasons lend balance to our climate. Victorians embraced the regeneration that came with spring, the plush green of summer, and the culmination of the growing season with the fall harvest. In particular, the press tracked the extreme heat, thunderstorms, tornadoes, floods, and droughts that accompanied seasonal change. Readers were especially treated to accounts of freakish weather, such as downpours of amphibians, heavenly bombardments of hailstones, and deadly strikes of lightning. In addition, Victorian Canadians marvelled at other natural phenomena, including meteor showers, earthquakes, and the Northern Lights. Of course, like us today, our forebears longed to discover the perfect forecasting technique, even if it sported a coat of fur or feathers.

During a thunderstorm on Thursday the 8th, two sheep were killed in this village by the lightning.

Huntingdon Canadian Gleaner, August 16, 1867

The sun enters Aries today, and spring, according to the almanac makers, commences. We shall be pleased to learn that these gentlemen are correct and trust that the virgin season will be modest sufficiently to prevent old winter lingering in her lap, as the poets say he sometimes does.

Halifax Acadian Recorder, March 21, 1868

A large water spout made its appearance on Georgian Bay on Wednesday last. It burst on the shore without doing any damage.

Hamilton Evening Times, August 17, 1868

The maple sugar makers in most parts of the district are loud in their complaints against the weather clerk for the "mean sugar weather" he is dealing out to them. Keep cool, honest John! The "sap" will run shortly.

Granby Gazette, April 8, 1870

On Sunday afternoon last during a heavy thunderstorm, frogs, from one-half to one inch in length, fell in heaps by the thousands near the Eagle Hotel and Newmarket train depot. The storm came from the north and the theory is that the "French staple" must have been twisted out of the Holland River Marsh by an eddying whirlwind. We observe by the Belleville Intelligencer that a like phenomenon occurred in the vicinity of that town.

Newmarket Era, July 1, 1870

There was a slight shock of an earthquake felt in this city Tuesday evening a little before 8 o'clock.

Fredericton Colonial Farmer, January 15, 1872

A son of Mr. Neil McArthur, who lives about 3 miles north of Wallacetown, was instantly killed by lightning last Monday morning about 10 o'clock. He was sitting on a chair with his head leaning against the wall when the house was struck. His right cheek, breast, abdomen and legs were discolored, and his hair was singed. On the floor where his feet were resting, were 2 holes, as if bullets had passed through. The funeral, which took place on Tuesday, was largely attended, and much sympathy was shown to the bereaved parents. The boy was 11 years of age.

St. Thomas Journal, July 18, 1873

The continued northeaster has caused a very heavy sea, preventing northern crafts from leaving here for their respective homes. It has also brought an unusual visitor at this time of the year in the shape of an iceberg.

St. John's Public Ledger, November 12, 1875

Tracadie was visited by a very serious hail storm on Monday of last week. The hail stones were as large as pigeons' eggs and in their descent broke windows and beat down grain and other growing crops.

Alberton Pioneer, August 26, 1876

A most beautifully tinted meteor shot across the sky last night at about ten o'clock. The scene was one of transcendent beauty.

Ottawa Citizen, November 10, 1877

Prairie fires illuminated the sky in every direction at night in the early part of last week, and clouds of smoke overhung the town. The rain of Wednesday night, however, checked its course, which was alarmingly close to the government buildings.

Saskatchewan Herald, April 21, 1879

For some time past the heat has been very intense. There were a great number of sunstrokes throughout the country, and a great many took sick and had to give up work.

St. Mary's Argus, July 28, 1881

Northern Lights - A grand display of auroral lights was witnessed on Sunday night. Beautiful colors, charmingly blended, made a magnificent picture of the heavens, and as the weather was mild and pleasant, the sight was fully enjoyed by promenaders. The modern explanation of the phenomenon attributes it to currents of electricity.

Collingwood Enterprise, April 20, 1882

The weather, to say the least, for the past month has not been encouraging either to farmers or merchants. The prospects for an early spring are no longer indulged. Yet who remembers a season without something to vex and annoy? The seed time is sure to come, and the only thing to do is wait and have patience.

Fredericton Evening Capital, May 17, 1884

Astronomers say the Star of Bethlehem is now visible in the east every morning, and it will not be visible again for 400 years. It can be seen at about 4 of the clock.

Alliston Weekly Herald, November 14, 1884

A miniature tornado was, yesterday, observed on Prince Street near Quirk's Bakery. A passing cloud seemed to suck up the dust from the street, and after circling around for a few moments, went whirling off dust and all, leaving a plainly discernable track. Fortunately, no "cyclone cellars" were necessary.

Charlottetown Daily Examiner, May 19, 1886

The hot sun of Saturday last, followed by the rain in the

morning, put great growth in the ground. Farmers say the wheat crop shot up more than an inch in the one day.

Morden Monitor, May 5, 1887

Tuesday last was one of, if not the hottest day of this season. The thermometer registered 131 [Fahrenheit] in the shade, which is almost enough to make one sigh for a young Dakota blizzard.

Prince Albert Times, July 13, 1888

Captain Trennery of the steamer Queensmore, who arrived at Baltimore a short time since, reports: "Off the Newfoundland Banks a phenomenon was witnessed, it being nothing more or less than a rain of blood apparently. It covered the decks, bridge, masts, smoke stacks, lifeboats, and every exposed part of the ship. When it came down, it was of a dark rich colour like human blood, but it soon dried up and assumed the colour of bird dust. All hands were badly scared and feared that a serious accident would happen. Captain Inch of the Rossmore also witnessed the same remarkable sight. No one can account for it. It was blowing very hard at the time."

Trinity Weekly Record, March 1, 1890

A rural weather prophet says the fact that the muskrats are leaving their holes and making for higher ground is a sure sign of a high freshet this spring.

Caledonia Gold Hunter & Farmers' Journal, March 28, 1891

We would respectfully request the Township Council to adopt a resolution to abolish the dry weather.

Jarvis Record, July 1, 1891

So intense was the heat on Tuesday that it actually hatched

out a chicken in the store of Coats and Son. This may seem improbable, but it is nevertheless a fact. Clinton New Era.

Jarvis Record, July 8, 1891

The Fort Benton River Press says that spring is at hand as a flock of ducks was seen flying over the town with their baggage checked for Saskatchewan.

Brandon Mail, February 18, 1892

Hot! At 95 degrees [Fahrenheit] in the shade in the "cool of the evening" (5 p.m.), few people care to work very hard.

Saskatchewan Herald, August 4, 1893

Everyone in town is speculating how high the floods will reach, but it is generally agreed that the Nelson and Fort Sheppard train depot is safe for the present.

Nelson Miner, June 2, 1894

The long, continued dry weather is having a serious effect on the root and corn crops. Farmers complain of a scarcity of water and a number have to draw it long distances. Many cheese factories in Western Ontario have been compelled to shut down. Suitable food for cows has become so scarce that the yield of milk has enormously decreased. Some cows, indeed, have become almost dry. For weeks farmers have been feeding hay to their cows and now special feed has to be given to sheep and pigs two months before the usual time. the result will be a run on hay that must materially decrease the stores for winter use.

Dutton Advance, August 30, 1894

Last week's storm was very destructive to fishermen's gear on the southern coast of this island. The fall run of mackerel were making their appearance and the fishermen had their nets out, but the storm of Tuesday and Wednesday carried nearly all the nets away. Not only have the nets been lost, but many barrels of fine mackerel, which otherwise would have been captured, will be lost to the fishermen. This is very unfortunate for the fishermen, as the season up to date has been a poor one.

North Sydney Herald, November 14, 1894

Mr. W.H. Patrick, who, it will be remembered, was struck by lightning some time ago, was in town last week on his way back to work for the Cochrane ranch. He seems to be fully recovered from his accident, but complains of a slight weakness of the eyes.

Lethbridge News, September 25, 1895

One hundred and four degrees [Fahrenheit] in the shade at Revelstoke.

Calgary Herald, July 17, 1899

Chapter Six

A Dangerous World

If the press of a century ago is an accurate gauge, our ancestors surely lived in a world where the danger of physical harm lurked around every corner. Like modern television newscasts, nineteenth-century newspapers routinely tallied the local accident toll. Editors devoted plenty of column space to reports about fires, poisonings, chokings, falls, work-related injuries, and animal bites. More sensational were pieces on gunfire mishaps, gas explosions, and gruesomely misplaced axe blows. Despite such stories, it is unlikely that the Victorians were anymore accident-prone than we are. After all, our world is filled with news reports about the bodily injury that our neighbours suffer. On this score, it would seem that we have inherited our obsessive fascination with the misfortunes of others. Have we done so because it is in our nature, or has generation after generation simply wished to break the monotony of the humdrum safeness that usually characterizes the routine of daily life?

Last evening while services were being conducted in St. Luke's Cathedral, a lighted match, thrown from the gallery, fell into the pew of His Excellency the Lieutenant-Governor and upon the dress of a lady sitting there. There was some little confusion at the moment, but the match was extinguished before any serious damage resulted. A young lad sitting in the gallery was fixed upon as the offender, and admitted to the act, stating that it was accidental. The matter awaits the action of the Church wardens. Had the match, one of the German fuse sort, fallen among the spruce on a flammable dress, there is no telling how terrible the result may have been.

Halifax Acadian Recorder, February 22, 1868

Poisoned by a Bug - One evening, about a week ago, Miss Maria Burkholder, a young lady about 18 years of age, daughter of Henry Burkholder of Binbrook, came home late from a party, and being thirsty, took a drink from a pail of water in the kitchen. She immediately discovered that she had heedlessly swallowed some object that had been in the water. A few minutes afterwards she was seized with a deathly sickness, her sight failed, her face and throat were distorted and swollen, and her tongue protruded from her mouth, while she seemed to suffer excruciating agony. Dr. Haney was called, and on learning the facts, administered a powerful emetic, which had the desired effect of ejecting from her stomach a large poisonous bug of a green color, such as is frequently seen in stagnant pools in the country. Miss Burkholder began improving immediately afterwards and is now almost wholly recovered. Hamilton Times.

Durham Chronicle, March 3, 1870

Frightful Accident - As two sons of Mr. James Fargue were engaged in extracting stumps in a field on the 8th instant, one brother stumbled forward and received a blow from the axe in the hands of the other. The blade had opened the right side of the head, cleaving the skull and penetrating the brain. Although the injury is of the most dangerous nature, Dr. N.O. Walker has fair hopes of his ultimate recovery.

Simcoe British Canadian, May 24, 1876

The origin of the fire in Detective Banning's house today is attributed to a mouse which got into the detective's vest pocket and nibbled away at some matches until it ignited them. It will now be in order for the detective to arrest his mouseship for incendiarism.

Ottawa Citizen, November 12, 1877

A farmer named Gillet, while passing through the Nelsonville saw mill, stumbled, and to save himself from falling, caught hold of a saw, which he mistook to be motionless. The saw being in motion, however, nearly cut through his hand. Dr. Rook was called and skillfully dressed the injured member.

Emerson International, January 30, 1879

Narrow Escape - Mr. Joseph Sibson, bookkeeper at Russell's Brewery, narrowly escaped being shot last Tuesday night. Sometime after midnight he was aroused by the crash of glass in his bedroom and by a sound as if a pistol had been discharged close to the building. An examination of the premises showed that a bullet had been fired through the window and had lodged in the foot of the bed in a direct line with where he had been sleeping. Had the aim been slightly higher, the shot would have taken effect upon the occupant of the bed. Mr. Sibson is at a loss to account for the affair. Appearances favor the idea that the shot was fired deliberately and with intention of doing him injury, and yet he cannot conceive who could owe him such a deadly grudge or what the motive could be. It is possible, however, that the shot was fired accidently or that it was aimed at some other object.

Sarnia Observer, April 25, 1879

Last week a lad in the Uxbridge school named Herbert Summerville got his finger taken off by getting it caught in the school door. The piece was cut clear off and dropped to the floor when the door was opened.

Woodville Advocate, January 6, 1881

An accident of a very peculiar character to the person of Mr. James Gray of Garden Hill occurred a few days ago. While Mr. Gray was in the barn yard, one of his horses ran up to him and bit off a large portion of his ear. The injured organ is doing as well as possible under the circumstances.

Woodville Advocate, January 6, 1881

Poisoned by Mistake - A sad event occurred at the village of Wardsville on Tuesday afternoon last. Dr. Gordon of that place, being sick, took what he supposed was a dose of medicine, but inadvertently swallowed a quantity of strychnine, which is a deadly poison. On the error being discovered, he took a large dose of chloroform, which undoubtedly saved his life, and medical aid was at once sent for. He is out of danger and improving favorably.

Bothwell Times, February 7, 1884

A Windsor, Ontario telegram says: "During a performance in a side show connected with John Harris' nickel-plated show, which exhibited in Windsor Saturday, a female artist, who was advertised as Mrs. Jesse James, while making a display of fancy shooting, missed her aim. The bullet, which was intended for a target, tore its way through the tent canvas and entered the breast of John Martini, a French farmer who lives a few miles out of Windsor. The bullet was a small one shot from a 32-calibre air rifle. Dr. Casgrain attended the injured man, but was unable to find the bullet. The doctor does not think the wound will be followed by serious results unless inflammation should set in."

Brussels Post, May 8, 1885

Narrow Escape from Drowning - Alexander Morrison, blacksmith of Upper Settlement, Baddeck, was attempting to cross on stilts the Baddeck River on Friday last at Neil McKay's farm. When in the middle of the river, the current proved too string for his artificial feet and carried his pins from under him, throwing Mr. Morrison into the water. By continued struggling, he gained the bank almost exhausted. Mr. Morrison is around again, and appears none the worse for his ducking.

Baddeck Island Reporter, April 8, 1886

Everett, son of Mrs. D. Hawkes of Caron, had a very close call last Saturday. His brother, Corda, was handling a revolver, when it accidently discharged, the bullet striking Everett behind the left ear, inflicting an ugly wound. Dr. Turnbull was at once sent for, but on his arrival, he found that the bullet could not be extracted. It had struck the base of the skull, glanced off, and imbedded itself deep in the fleshy portion of the neck. The wound, although painful, is not dangerous and the lad is doing as well as could be expected under the circumstances.

Moose Jaw Times, November 7, 1890

Experience Teaches - A mounted policeman named Thompson had a rather painful experience last Sunday evening. Passing by the shed above the gas well, pipe in mouth, he thoughtlessly put his head through the open door. The building was full of gas, which igniting, caused an explosion which threw Mr. Thompson back several feet from the entrance. His face was badly burned. A moment afterwards the building was in flames, and the crowd which quickly gathered extinguished with difficulty the escaping gas after the shack had burned to the ground. Medicine Hat Times.

Macleod Gazette, August 20, 1891

Hampton Notes - A little daughter of John Riley, while attempting to get a pail of water from the well, lost her balance and fell head first into the well, a distance of 12 feet. The little one escaped almost miraculously without much injury, receiving, however, some bad bruises. Fortunately, there were only a few inches of water in the well. The little thing climbed out without assistance. She is now on the fair road to recovery, the shock being the worst part of the accident.

King's County News, December 13, 1894

Elgin Notes - Mr. James Wheaton's little daughter was kicked by a horse Saturday night and had three teeth knocked out.

King's County News, June 20, 1895

As a wagon loaded with a German family and household goods was passing the Manitoba Hotel yesterday, a little girl fell from it and the wheels passed over her. Her throat was completely lacerated, but she showed no signs of grief. She was picked up, put into the wagon, and the party drove on as if nothing had happened, the mules waving their ears philosophically as they picked their way along the high spots in the Main Street pavement.

Winnipeg Free Press, July 7, 1896

Abbotsford News - Miss Vivian Gibb met with an accident the other day by running into a wagon team on her "bike."

Granby Mail, November 7, 1896

Arthur Charlton of St. Thomas met with a very serious accident recently while splitting wood. The axe hit the clothesline and came back on him with sufficient force as to cause an ugly wound.

Stratford Daily Beacon, January 3, 1899

Middle River News - J.W. Campbell, Esquire, of the west side met with a painful, though not dangerous accident recently. He had been chopping some wood, when a chip flew from the axe and struck him on the mouth, making an ugly gash and breaking one of his front teeth.

Baddeck Telephone, March 1, 1899

Bitten by a Tarantula - Miss Nettie Brownlee, a Kemptville young lady, was bitten on the hand a few days ago by a tarantula while she was taking bananas from a large bunch in one of the stores there. The hand immediately began to swell from the effects of the bite and it was feared at one time that it was poisoned so severely that the arm would have to be amputated. By prompt attention, however, the serious effect was averted.

Merrickville Star, July 6, 1899

Chapter Seven

Matters Medical

Although journalists may have overplayed their coverage of accidents, they, in a reasonably accurate light, reflected Canadians' concerns about health issues. In an age when epidemics of influenza, diphtheria, cholera, small pox, and typhus could sweep across the entire country almost unchecked, and when distance, transportation, and cost made immediate medical attention an impractical luxury for most, it is not surprising that the fear of sickness was omnipresent in Victorian society. Consequently, newspapers were quick to comment upon what particular communicable maladies were plaguing a given area, to chronicle public initiative to fight disease, and to broadcast hope by printing home remedies and detailing the accomplishments of the medical community. Of course, quackery and incredibly outrageous claims (to our ears at least) also crept into the realm of nineteenth-century health care. Then again, are we not still searching for that magic elixir to cure all that ails us?

Cholera - A certain cure of this disease may be found in the use of Perry Davis' Pain Killer.

Montreal Gazette, July 3, 1867

Owing to a pile of diseased coffin boards kept near the old cemetery, the people in that neighbourhood are sickening.

Quebec Morning Chronicle, July 9, 1867

HINTS ON SEA-BATHING - Invalids should be prevented from bathing before breakfast. But due time must be allowed for the digestion of the meal, as any strong impression on the mind or body is liable to arrest or destroy digestion; therefore, two hours should elapse after breakfast and after dinner, before the bath is taken. The patient must be directed to plunge at one into the water, and not to stand shivering for some time until the surface of the body is cooled. He should slip down and allow each wave to pass completely over him. It is the temperature of the sea to which we must have regard when we give directions to patients at what time of the year they may bathe with advantage. If the patient is not much debilitated, the months of May and September are good, and they should choose a shore on which the billows are rough. If, on the other hand, the patient be weak and depressed, the summer months are preferable, and a calm sea should be chosen. - Medical Times.

Quebec Daily News, July 26, 1867

The teeth in the insane are prone to undergo certain changes. Dr. Langdon Down, who read a paper on this subject before the Odontological Society, states therein that from an examination of nearly a thousand cases, he has found that he could, in the majority of instances, state the period at which the imbecility or insanity began.

Quebec Mercury, July 2, 1872

The vandal agents of quack medicine men have been disfiguring the walls and buildings of Moncton in the most shameless manner. All the new posts of the Dominion Telegraph Company on Main Street are covered with their placards.

Moncton Daily Times, August 13, 1877

Diphtheria continues to spread in the outlying districts. It is rife in Middle Musquodoboit - Mr. John D. Tupper has lost a son, aged 13, from the disease.

Halifax Evening Reporter, February 19, 1879

REMARKABLE OPERATION - An operation requiring the greatest of surgical skill was successfully performed by Drs. Harvey & Stanley, of Watford, assisted by Drs. A. Harvey and Newell, of Wyoming, and Mr. Symington, student of Dr. A. Harvey, in the removal of an ovarian tumor weighing over 40 pounds from the abdomen of Mrs. A. Gilroy, Brooke [Township], on the 1st of October. A case in surgery of this kind is rare and its successful performance reflects great credit on these gentlemen. Nine days have now passed since the operation, and Mrs. Gilroy is fast recovering, and a valuable life has been saved by the operation.

Watford Guide-News, October 10, 1879

Good medical authority says the habit of eating snow and ice induces catarrh by chilling the thin partition forming the roof of the mouth and the floor of the nostrils, thus causing congestion.

Bedford Times, February 9, 1883

An insane person, who has been confined in the town jail for the past month, was removed yesterday to the Insane Asylum at Dartmouth. The cart provided to take him on the Strait was hardly fit for a dog, let alone a human being. It was a disgrace to the community that anyone, even an insane person, should be so treated.

Baddeck Island Reporter, April 1, 1886

A lady residing on the Elora road received a letter a short time ago from her sister, who lives in Fergus, and who had just recovered from a severe attack of diphtheria. Being busy at the time and having both hands occupied, she placed the corner of the letter in her mouth until she could free her hands to read it. The next day she complained of a sore throat, and a few days afterwards the doctor informed her she had contracted diphtheria. The above goes to show how careful persons should be in communicating with anyone suffering from a contagious disease.

Shelburne Economist, December 9, 1886

The influenza has been making great havoc at the police barracks. It is said that twenty or more of the officers and men have been down at one time. Supt. McIllree himself was attacked while at Banff a few days ago.

Calgary Herald, January 9, 1890

The Board of Health will meet tonight and decide what is to be done with Shilson, the occupant of the small pox hospital. The patient has anything but the appearance of a sick man. He and Wilson, his nurse, are out daily exercising themselves at baseball and by the time of their release they will be in condition to take a position as battery on some professional ball team.

Sarnia Observer, May 1, 1891

Mr. Lewis Bentley, representing the enterprising firm of T. Milburn & Co., manufacturers of proprietary medicines, Toronto, was in town this week and left a mark of his visit on every electric light pole and on every fence.

Regina Standard, June 26, 1891

Celery coffee is a new drink. It is said to give renewed strength to the brain and nerves.

Sudbury Journal, January 5, 1893

The probabilities are that our school board will pass a resolution compelling all children to produce a certificate of vaccination before entering the schools at their opening.

Wallaceburg Herald, July 27, 1894

Hampton Notes - We notice that a house near the station is placarded as containing scarlet fever, yet we notice that the boys of the family run around the streets the same as usual. We do not wish to pose as an alarmist, but we do think that as other people have children that those in authority should see to it that these boys are not allowed to run at large any sooner than perfect safety permits.

King's County News, November 29, 1894

Dandruff forms when the glands of the skin are weakened, and if neglected, baldness is sure to follow. Hall's Hair Renewer is the best preventive.

Guysboro Gazette, August 2, 1895

Dr. Agnew, of this city, put in an artificial eye a few days ago for H. Gale, who lives near Carberry. He attended the hospital here for some time suffering from a wound in the eye he received from a chip while chopping wood. The substituted eye and a recovered man are the result.

Brandon Mail, February 13, 1896

Measles are still prevalent in the city. During the past week 33 cases were reported to the medical health officer. The other cases reported were diphtheria 14, scarlet fever 3, and typhoid 1, making a total of 51. During the corresponding week last year there were only 3 cases, all of scarlet fever.

Winnipeg Free Press, July 6, 1896

The contagious disease building at the general hospital is filled with patients and it is with great difficulty that any more patients can be accommodated.

Winnipeg Free Press, July 8, 1896

There are twenty cases of typhoid in Woodstock. Well water is given as the cause. In one case where a girl died of the disease twelve dead toads were taken from the well out of which water was used by her family. This should induce our citizens to see that their wells are cleaned out.

Alvinston Free Press, August 30, 1899

Chapter Eight

Death

Death is an inescapable fact of life. Such is the case now, and it was certainly the case a century ago. Sadly, nineteenth-century Canadians lived in a world where dying was an all too familiar occurrence. Insufficient medical knowledge and malnutrition robbed countless parents of their bundles of joy. Occupational accidents frequently snatched the living from fellow workers, friends, and family. And disease, that mighty leveller of all people, indiscriminately struck down the weak and the strong, the young and the old, and the rich and the poor. Indeed, life-expectancy rates before 1900 were at least twenty to twenty-five years lower than they are now. Octogenarians were quite rare, and centenarians were virtually unheard of.

Probably because of the great mystery surrounding the eternal voyage, Victorian Canadians held a morbid fascination for death. Therefore, it should come as no surprise that reports about ethereal departures filled their newspapers. Given the pervasiveness of dying, a significant portion of this commentary was very matter-of-fact or quite abrupt. Journalists generally reserved their more detailed and macabre descriptions for unusual or downright peculiar expirations or for the deaths of prominent individuals. In addition, they generally saved their most melancholy tones for the tragic passings of the young.

Burials [from cholera deaths] last week rose to the alarming number of 144. Only 18 were adults.

Quebec Morning Chronicle, July 9, 1867

One of the laborers connected with DeHaven's Circus, while sleeping on top of one of the cars, rolled off near Trenton and was killed. He was not missed until the train reached Trenton, and on parties going back, the body was found lying near the side of the track, and from the fact of the grass being torn up for some distance around the body, it is evident he had lived for some time after being thrown off.

Belleville Intelligencer, July 30, 1867

Last Saturday, the 9th instant, a heavy southerly storm committed great havoc in the harbor of St. John. In the evening, the brigantine Bessie, in entering the harbor, struck the rocks, the captain was lost overboard, and the vessel having lost its rudder, drifted to the eastern shore under the Alms House. Bt the great exertions of the pilot, Mr. Mullin, and Captain Frith, the crew of seven were rescued from their perilous position on the wreck. The body of Captain Tobin was subsequently found and buried with Masonic honors.

Halifax Acadian Recorder, February 22, 1868

Fatal Accident in New Brunswick - A young man named Titus Parker, while skating on the Kennebeccasis River on Sunday last, fell through the ice and was drowned. He was returning from a funeral at the time.

Halifax Novascotian, December 21, 1868

Fatal Accident at Strathroy - An accident of a very distressing nature occurred at the races at Strathroy on the 24th, whereby a young lad named Robinson, aged about fifteen years, son of Mr. F. Robinson, hotel-keeper of Komoka, lost his life. He was chosen to ride a horse in one of the races, and shortly after starting, the animal bolted and ran amongst some trees. Young Robinson, being an inexperienced rider, lost all control of his horse, and his head coming in contact with the projecting limb of a tree, his neck was broken, and he died almost instantly. This event put an end to the sport, and cast gloom over the subsequent proceedings.

London Free Press, May 26, 1869

On Wednesday last, a child of Mr. Japp, wagon maker of Douglas, Garafraxa Township, swallowed a button with which it had been playing. The button stuck in the child's throat and could neither be moved up nor down. Three physicians were in attendance and it was resolved to cut the windpipe. This was done, but the child's life could not be saved.

Guelph Advertiser, January 27, 1870

Captain John Rabbits, of the schooner Jane, arrived at this port, reports having seen on March 16 the schooner Thorwalsden of Gloucester bottom up and sails set.

St. John's Morning Chronicle, May 1, 1873

Two men, John Potts and John Jackson, fell down the pump shaft at the Albion Mines on Saturday last and were instantly killed. A chain broke and precipitated the men to the bottom, a distance of 900 feet.

Amherst Maritime Sentinel, August 20, 1874

A young man named Briggs fell from the topmast of a vessel at Liverpool, Nova Scotia on Thursday last and was instantly killed.

Cape Breton Advocate, April 15, 1875

A new hearse of modern and handsome build and fashion has been imported by Mr. J.R. Tupper, Jr. While commending the enterprise, we can only hope that the hearse will have more employment as an object of curiosity in Mr. Tupper's livery stable than for its legitimate yet melancholy purpose.

Carleton Sentinel, May 15, 1875

The daughter of Mr. William Moore, St. John, fell down the stairs in Vernon's building, King Street, broke her skull and died in a few hours.

Moncton Daily Times, August 15, 1877

A man was nearly eaten up by a bear near Alberton last week. They could find but fragments of his body.

Prince Edward Island Farmer, August 7, 1878

At Athlone recently, an occurrence of a melancholy character occurred. A boy named Burke, while delivering bread at the Athlone barracks, was plagued by a soldier named Dawes of the 75th Regiment. The lad appeared much annoyed at Dawes, and lifting a bread knife lying on the table, threatened the soldier with it if the soldier did not stop annoying him. He flourished the knife in his hand, and in doing so the blade left the handle and penetrated the soldier's breast to the heart, and he died in about ten minutes. Burke was afterwards given into custody of the police, but at the inquest, it being shown that the occurrence was purely accidental, he was released.

Chatham [New Brunswick] *Gleaner*, December 14, 1878

Peculiar Death - The Uxbridge Guardian of last week has the following paragraph: "About 2 weeks ago, a fine, healthy-looking young man named William H. McMullen, residing on the 8th Concession of Whitchurch, had occasion to have a tooth drawn, and strange to say, up to the time of his death, which melancholy event took place on Christmas Day, he bled profusely from the mouth and nose."

Owen Sound Advertiser, January 15, 1880

Shocking Death - A sailor named T. Pollard, a native of Poplar, England, was burned to death at Nanaimo on July 1st. He had been temporarily chained by a policeman to a post in a stable, and the stable catching fire, the poor fellow was burned to death in spite of every effort to free him. His cries for help were most heartrending.

Kamloops Inland Sentinel, July 8, 1880

As the mail train was coming west on Friday evening, a fatal accident occurred near Shedden. A farmer by the name of I. Lammy and his hired man were crossing the track on a sleigh when the rear bob on which Lammy was seated was struck by the engine, throwing him about twenty feet and mangling him terribly. The engineer saw that there was about to be a catastrophe and blew the whistle of the engine, but the hired man was quite deaf and did not notice it. It is surprising that Lammy did not notice the approaching train in time to avoid the accident. People cannot be too careful in looking out for approaching trains before crossing railway tracks. On Monday an inquest was to be held, but it was adjourned till Friday.

Dutton Enterprise, January 1, 1885

Canada lost $1,568,728 and 69 lives by marine casualties last year.

Charlottetown Daily Examiner, March 20, 1886

Andrew Ball, aged 13, a Delhi farmer's son, died as the result of injury to his spine sustained by falling back on a stone.

Norwich Gazette, August 9, 1888

A man named William Hutchings was accidently killed at Spaniard's Bay on Thursday. He fell while carrying wood on his shoulder, and the wood fractured his skull.

Trinity Weekly Record, February 15, 1890

A logger named Thomas Michaud, in the employ of the Hastings Saw Mill Co. of Vancouver, was killed in the woods on Valdez Island a few days ago by a falling tree. His head was crushed into a pulp and death was instantaneous.

Chilliwack Progress, June 25, 1891

Frozen to Death - One of the saddest accidents in the history of the North-West happened last week near Medicine Hat. Two boys, the sons of Messrs. Cochrane and Walton of Medicine Hat, left that place on Friday last to drive some cattle to the Cypress Hills. It was a beautiful morning when they started out, but the blizzard which set in in the afternoon, and which was much more severe there than it was here, came up suddenly and they were caught in it. As they did not turn up, search was made for them, with the result that both boys were found frozen to death.

Macleod Gazette, November 26, 1891

It is worth your while to take a walk down 7th Street to the "Excelsior Marble Works," and see the assortment of all kinds of extra tombstones and monuments, which are already prepared to mark the resting places of some peoples' "loved ones."

Brandon Mail, January 29, 1892

Michael Brandt, Berlin, dropped dead last Friday while splitting wood. He was road commissioner and was about 60 years of age. Heart failure was the cause.

Waterloo County Chronicle, January 25, 1894

James Simmons of Sarnia Township, while driving cattle to water, was attacked by a bull and thrown into the air. He fell heavily on his head and lived only a few minutes, his neck having been broken.

Dutton Advance, August 30, 1894

Hampton Notes - A very sad accident occurred at the Village on Sunday morning, which resulted in the death of a bright little child, Grace Seely, aged about seven. The little one got up Sunday morning and went downstairs to the fire to get warm before dressing, and in some way her night dress caught fire, and the little one was considerably burned. The fire is supposed to have penetrated her lungs. Drs. Warneford and Smith were summoned and did all they could for the little sufferer, but their efforts were unavailing, as at an early hour in the evening, after great suffering, the little one passed away. The child was a daughter of the late Edward Seely, and her untimely death has cast a gloom over the community. The mother and family are tendered the sympathy of the people in their sad affliction.

King's County News, January 10, 1895

Patrick Ready, aged 22, a farm hand near St. Catharines, was impaled on an iron upright on his hay wagon. It entered his hip and came out at his mouth. He is dead.

Alexandria Glengarrian, July 26, 1895

Mr. and Mrs. J.M. Chisholm of 38 Lily Street mourn the death of their youngest child, aged 13 months, who died suddenly Saturday afternoon from sunstroke. The funeral takes place this afternoon.

Winnipeg Free Press, July 13, 1896

D.M. Mitchell, our popular furniture man, left by train on Monday for Toronto to attend an embalming school, as there is also a large furniture exposition at the present time in Toronto. "Dexter" will likely keep his eyes open for pointers in his line.

Granby Mail, September 2, 1896

Alex Easton, 18 years old, died Monday afternoon from

injuries received by a fall down the shaft of the Le Roi mine about a week ago. His leg, thigh, and jaw were broken, and he was severely bruised otherwise. He fell about 75 feet. The remains lie at the home of his parents near the City of Spokane mine. Mr. Easton came from Youngstown, Ohio, and his remains may be taken there for burial.

Rossland Weekly Miner, November 18, 1897

A young man named Baker, while grain threshing at Mr. C. Asselstine's farm, North Fredericksburgh [Twp.], on Monday, stepped into the cylinder. His right foot and leg were badly crushed to the knee. The limb was amputated, but the shock was too serious, death occurring on Tuesday morning.

Napanee Beaver, August 12, 1898

While Thomas Lally of Chatham was walking in the woods near that city on Sunday, his dogs discovered the body of a headless man. Upon making an examination of the ground in the vicinity, a black felt hat was found, but not the head. An outfit for repairing was found near the body, which would indicate that the body found was that of an itinerant umbrella mender. Coroner Bray was at once notified, and he decided to hold an inquest. Nothing could be found in the pockets that could throw any light on the dead man's identity. The police are investigating this probable murder.

Blenheim News, August 18, 1898

Chapter Nine

At Play

Doom and gloom did not cast a dark shadow over every aspect of life in Victorian Canada. Quite spirited, our antecedents shared a great sense of communal play and revelled in a variety of games, sports, and social events. Gatherings, such as spelling bees, masquerades, card matches, club meetings, and strawberry socials, afforded endless opportunity for neighbourly interaction. In an age of increasing leisure time, sport allowed those so inclined to test and prove their physical capabilities. Across the country, boxers, billiard players, bicyclists, rowers, wood-choppers, road-racers, cricketers, curlers, baseball teams, and lacrosse squads competed for mere local bragging rights all the way up to much coveted regional and national championships. As an interesting aside, it was not until the end of the century that formally organized ice hockey began its march to the forefront of our athletic imagination. The Victorians also had at their disposal a host of other amusements, including everything from the circus to fortune-telling. Above all, however, these social diversions served to reinforce a sense of community, and by commenting upon such activities, nineteenth-century scribes helped to forge this spirit.

We are glad to see that the billiards fever among our Montreal amateurs has not abated. Almost every evening a match takes place in Messrs. Dions' private rooms. Some of these matches show very good play. The last match on Saturday evening between Messrs. B. and L., two well known amateurs, was won by the former. Score 580 to 437; average 4½; best run 45.

Montreal Gazette, July 10, 1867

The Timber Slides - During the last few days quite a number of ladies - strangers in the city, and bent on seeing all the sights - have been going through the slides on the timber cribs. Despite the wet feet incident to the affair, most of the gentle ones seem highly delighted with the novel sensation and express themselves well pleased with the rough, honest nature of their voyageur crew.

Ottawa Citizen, July 12, 1867

DE HAVEN'S IMPERIAL CIRCUS - This circus visits Belleville on Monday, the 29th inst. - Accompanying this circus are the LaFontaine brothers, the accomplished gymnasts, Mrs. Oliver Bell, the great female equestrian, "La Petite Annie," the most graceful and dexterous tight rope performer of her age now travelling, Mr. Dutton, the champion rider and leaper, and many others. The press universally commend it as a first-class affair, managed in a spirit of liberality, and with an especial view to the tastes of the people.

Belleville Intelligencer, July 23, 1867

The baseball game played at Woodstock yesterday for the championship of Canada between the Young Canadians of that place and the Victoria Club of Ingersoll resulted in a victory for the former. Score, Young Canadians, 42; Victoria, 34

Hamilton Evening Times, August 20, 1868

A four-oared boat race came off yesterday between Lachapelle's "Amateur" and C. Levi's "Maple Leaf" for a wager of $50 per side. The course rowed was from the Dredger at James' Bay, round Dead Man's Island and back, a distance of 2½ miles. The Amateur won by over two lengths in just twenty minutes' time.

Victoria British Columbian, March 27, 1869

Whittling seems to be a common habit in all new countries. For lack of a chunk of wood, your habitual whittler will shave away at a frame building or a [wooden] sidewalk. Litigants and court spectators seem to be great whittlers, and the authorities of Richfield have considerately placed a cord of wood near the front of the court house for the accommodation of whittlers so that the building may not be completely destroyed.

Cariboo Sentinel, June 18, 1870

A foot race for $1000 and the championship of Canada took place in Toronto last Tuesday afternoon between Burgess of Woodstock and Bingham of Bradford, distance seventy-five yards, which was won by the latter.

Sherbrooke Gazette, October 1, 1870

The spelling mania, now so prevalent in the United States, has broken out in Whitby. A match is announced to take place at the rooms of the Young Men's Christian Association tomorrow evening for which no charge of admission will be made. An interesting time is expected.

Whitby Chronicle, April 15, 1875

All who are favorable toward Canada's great national game, and who are possessed of sufficient patriotism to advocate the establishment of a lacrosse club in Simcoe, are requested to attend a meeting at Cairn's Hotel tomorrow evening at half-past eight o'clock for the purposes of organizing a club.

Simcoe British Canadian, June 21, 1876

71

Rope jumping is now in vogue with little girls.

London Free Press, April 14, 1877

All Battleford suspended operations and turned out to witness a bare-back bronco race on Tuesday on the north side of Battle River. It was a half-mile dash for $10 against a bag of pemican, Donald McIvor naming Mr. Dickieson's Buckskin and the other horse being Basil Lafonde's sorrel. The sorrel horse won.

Saskatchewan Herald, December 2, 1878

The members of the St. George's Snow Shoe Club will have their usual tramp this evening. A large turnout is desired.

Winnipeg Daily Times, February 2, 1881

A sleight of hand man, ventriloquist, juggler, and otherwise accomplished itinerant stopped off here the other day and gave an exhibition of his skill in the mysterious arts. He formed a class of about a dozen and agreed for the small sum of twenty-five cents to impart to them all the secrets of his wonderful calling. He taught them some things of interest, card tricks, etc., but the next day he "took the first train west," and whether he intends to turn up again to give the class the balance of their 25 cts.' worth is a question of time.

St. Mary's Argus, July 28, 1881

Strawberries are very plentiful and strawberry festivals will, no doubt, be all the rage for the next few weeks.

Bridgewater Weekly Telephone, July 5, 1882

Harry Manley from Philadelphia intends shortly opening up a gymnasium in this city, and is meanwhile looking up a suitable place. Mr. Manley, we understand, has been trained in a hard school under Madden, of New York, Sullivan's trainer, and also under the tutorship of Prof. Baldwin, of Sydney. He intends giving lessons in boxing, sword-exercise, fencing and wrestling, and we have reason to believe that Mr. Manley is a *connoisseur* in these things.

Brandon Mail, January 12, 1883

Mr. Ferguson appeared on South Railway Street on a bicycle, the first one in Regina. Mr. F. rides remarkably well. We hope there will be a club here this coming summer.

Regina Leader, March 29, 1883

The Mounted Police cricket team vanquished the cricket team at Qu'Appelle. The Regina team vanquished the Mounted Police!

Regina Leader, July 12, 1883

A pool shark struck town last week and did the "slick" players up for many dollars. He assumed the dress and demeanor of a greenie.

Toronto World, February 2, 1885

While a young lad by the name of Wilmot, son of William Wilmot, of Alberta County, was fishing tom-a-cods yesterday in the river, he hauled one to the top of the water, when it was immediately seized by a large sea gull that was passing over. The boy's hook caught in the bird's bill and the youngster gallantly captured the pair.

Sydney Advocate, October 29, 1885

The new skating rink was opened on Tuesday evening last, we learn, under very favorable auspices. Skating is an enjoyable means of recreation for young persons and when not participated in to excess may prove a healthful exercise to those in sedentary occupations of life.

Twillingate Sun, January 30, 1886

Boxing is becoming quite a rage in the town. An athletic club has been formed, which meets in the hall over W.H. Taylor's grocery, for enjoying and learning the "manly art," as well as indulging in other athletic exercises. There are several excellent boxers in the club who have attained more than ordinary proficiency with the gloves.

Brant Review, April 16, 1886

The roller rink craze is dying out. Managers are "skipping out" and rinks are burning all over the continent.

Acton Free Press, June 3, 1886

The Odd Stockings of Limehouse and the Georgetown team had a game of baseball on Tuesday last. The score was 22 to 6 in favor of the Georgetown team. The 22 runs were made by the Georgetown umpire, not the team; but cheer up boys, the return match is coming. You will then have an umpire that will give due credit and no favor.

Acton Free Press, August 26, 1886

The steamer United Empire made a trip by moonlight around the islands in the bay. A large number took advantage of the opportunity. Lots of fun and a pleasant trip.

Fort William Journal, September 8, 1887

Sir John A. Macdonald [age 73] presided at the opening of a toboggan slide in Ottawa a few nights ago. He descended the slide and enjoyed the sport immensely.

Muskoka Herald, January 19, 1888

Lefroy News - The Churchill Curling Club sent two rinks to Aurora on Friday and vanquished the local club by 21 shots.

Bradford Witness, March 8, 1888

A number of gypsies are camped near the old show ground and are making money fortune telling.

Muskoka Herald, June 7, 1888

The Oshawa fire brigade won $100 in a tug-of-war at Sarnia last week.

Bowmanville Canadian Statesman, August 22, 1888

Some of the ladies of the town are endeavoring to get up a "Ladies Match" in the Saskatchewan Rifle Association meeting next month. We hope they will succeed and get not only one prize but several.

Prince Albert Times, July 27, 1888

About forty or fifty sports from London, Paris and Brantford held a cockfight north of the city last night. Five battles were fought, Brantford winning three of them and the main [one].

Brantford Daily Expositor, October 29, 1889

A grand masquerade carnival will be held in the Moose Jaw skating rink on Friday evening, Jan. 31st. Prizes will be given for the best lady's costume and the best gentleman's costume. Only masked skaters are allowed on the ice before 12 o'clock.

Moose Jaw Times, January 24, 1890

Isaac Wallace, of Sarnia, sawed a cord of green maple, one cut, at Exeter [Ontario] yesterday, beating John Westcott, of the latter place, winning $50, and retaining the championship of Canada. Time, 57 minutes.

Sarnia Observer, April 17, 1891

The first game of the Macleod Polo Club took place on Sample's bottom on Saturday evening. There is good material in the club, and a representative Macleod team will no doubt be able to hold its own with all comers.

Macleod Gazette, August 13, 1891

Mud and marbles have been making fun for small boys of late.

Thamesville Herald, February 4, 1892

Phonograph concerts were given here on Monday and Tuesday evenings of this week. Those present expressed themselves as being highly pleased.

Mildmay Gazette, June 29, 1893

Lawn tennis is again coming into favor with the ladies.

Saskatchewan Herald, August 4, 1893

The Norman checker players will go over to Rat Portage [now Kenora] to play another match with the Rodentia Club next Thursday night.

Kenora News, February 16, 1894

Another brother of Louis Cyr, the strong man, who at present lives in St. Boniface, Quebec, will follow his brother's example and travel as a strong man. He is only 19 years old, measuring 5 feet 9 inches, and weighing 156 pounds. He lifts 447 pounds with one finger and carries over 2,200 pounds on his back.

Port Elgin Times, April 25, 1894

Halifax has a hockey league of five clubs, who play under the rules of the Maritime Provinces' Athletic Association. Truly, the game is booming from one end of the country to the other, for in the far west they are also playing the game. In Halifax, off-side play is allowed.

Toronto Star, January 4, 1896

In the international skating races for the championship of the world, held at Montreal yesterday, Jack McCullough of Winnipeg won the 5,000 metre race in the fast time of 8 minutes, 2 and 4/5 seconds, beating the world's record by 5 seconds.

Alberta Tribune, February 6, 1897

Blenheim has a ladies' bicycle club.

Tilbury Times, May 6, 1898

A ladies' hockey club has been formed in St. Thomas. In case any local female septetters wish to contest for honors, they may be able to arrange a match by writing to the secretary, Miss Mary Laycock of St. Thomas.

Stratford Daily Beacon, January 6, 1899

Remember the wrestling match between Dick Tucker and Ben Trenneman at the Monte Carlo theatre next Friday evening. It will be a hummer, and decide the championship of the Yukon valley.

Yukon Sun, January 17, 1899

A new bicycle livery and repair shop has been opened by A. Trolley in connection with the shoe shop. Wheels can be rented for 10 cents per hour, or 65 cents per day. Repairs promptly done; charges moderate.

Alvinston Free Press, May 4, 1899

You will laugh and grow fat if you attend the opera house next Monday and Tuesday.

Calgary Herald, July 25, 1899

Bob Ward drops around occasionally, but since he won $2,800 at poker, the boys play shy of him and he has to busk the tiger to amuse himself.

Dawson Daily News, September 11, 1899

Chief Stewart is now the possessor of a wheel [bicycle], having bought the one that Capt. Bennett brought over the ice. The chief is prepared in 4 weeks' time to race anyone in Dawson any distance from grasshopper's jump to the Rocky Mountains.

Yukon Sun, March 27, 1900

Chapter Ten

Affairs of the Heart

While some might put forward the cases of hatred and violence, love, thankfully, is the true constant in human history. Cupid hardly spared nineteenth-century Canadians from his arrow. Indeed, press commentary from the period reveals a more passionate world than we often believe existed. Victorians went to great lengths to satisfy their romantic impulses. Some couples were so enamoured with each other that they eloped, in order to escape parental objections or to free themselves from existing spouses. Of course, wandering lovers often bore the scorn of their forsaken companions. Age gaps, too, were no barriers to union. However, May-to-December marriages often received a measure of social disapproval in the form of the cat-calling, pot-banging, and horn-tooting of a charivari. Newspapers assumed an active role in the drama of courtship. Besides printing wedding notices, marvelling at scandalous elopements, and generally remarking on the power of love, they also readily dispensed advice about the proper selection of a mate.

ELOPEMENT - On Saturday evening last a Mrs. Anderson, residing on Peel Street, absconded from the Hymenial roof in company with Edward Wright, the well known photographic artist and billiard player. The loving pair sighed to breathe the fresh air of "Freedom" in each other's society and hastened, not in the "ways of love," but on that more prosaic conveyance, the Great Western Railway train, towards the American frontier. Meanwhile, the forsaken husband, becoming aware of his loss and cognizant also of the absence of certain monies which were even more precious in his sight than his faithless wife, telegraphed to have the erring pair arrested at the Suspension Bridge. Not dreaming of danger, but with their minds filled with pleasant anticipation of a "course of true love" lying all smooth before them, Mr. Wright and his companion soon found themselves at the Suspension Bridge. In a few more minutes, the waters of Niagara would form a barrier between them and the man whom Wright had wronged. But alas for the unreliability of all human hopes, the blissful dream was abruptly ended by the appearance of an official who arrested them, and compelling them to leave the train, forced them to relinquish their cherished scheme of migration and detained them until the husband could be heard from. If it be true that Mrs. A. has taken any of her husband's property with her, we sincerely hope that he may recover it; as for her and Mr. Edward Wright, we do not imagine that it is of much consequence to the wronged husband or to the public in general whether they go or stay.

Hamilton Spectator, February 18, 1867

A lady advertising for a husband says she wants a full grown man. None under 6 feet need apply. A chance for one of our tall Truro boys.

Truro Advertiser, November 2, 1867

Friday was St. Valentine's Day, and we learn that many missions of the usual character passed through the post office on that day.

Unionist & Halifax Journal, February 17, 1868

Epidemic - The marrying and giving in marriage fever has broken out again in this town since Easter, and so many young folks are joining their fortunes together for better or worse that it would make your head swim to count them.

St. Catharines Evening Journal, April 12, 1872

A Charivari that didn't come off - Mr. R.R. Hall, of this village, has again taken to himself a wife - Mrs. Daly, of Kingston. The ceremony was performed at Kingston, and the newly married couple arrived home on Wednesday evening. Of course, a charivari was organized; this appears to be one of the barbarisms which civilization is unable to shake off or put down, and against which there is no protection. The mob assembled on Thursday night with their horns and pans, but Mr. Hall met them with a compromise, and liberal "treating" bought them off. Gananoque Reporter.

Kingston Daily News, September 22, 1873

Elopement - When the ship Cariboo-Fly reached the narrows below Nanaimo yesterday morning on the down trip, she was hailed by a canoe, which proved to contain a young man and woman of Nanaimo, who had eloped and were on the way to Victoria to get married. Captain Holmes took them on board and brought them to Victoria, where they were made happy at last.

Victoria British Colonist, March 17, 1877

Six and a half feet of bride stood before the altar in a Dundas Street church the other day, and promised to love, cherish and obey five feet of bridegroom; and that's the long and short of it.

London Free Press, June 2, 1877

Last night a girl name Alphosine Valade went out on a jamboree. Whilst roaming around Dalhousie Street, she met her lover with another girl. About five minutes later, somebody's hair ornamented the sidewalk, and a young man might be observed sitting in a mud hole. It wasn't Alphosine's hair; it was the other girl's, and the young man in the mud hole was the deceitful lover. The police came up whilst Alphosine was using some strong language and arrested her. She was committed for three months.

Ottawa Citizen, November 15, 1877

Don't sit between the window and the light when you are kissing your girl, especially if the curtains are white. It makes other people envious.

Chatham [Ontario] *Tri-Weekly Planet*, November 20, 1878

Girls Beware! - Girls beware of transient young men. Never suffer the addresses of a stranger. Recollect that one good farmer's boy or an industrious mechanic is worth all the floating tops in the world. The allurements of a dandy Jack, with a gold chain round his neck, a walking stick in his paw, a threepenny cigar in his mouth, or some honest tailor's coat on his back, and a brainless, though fancy skull, never can make up the loss of a good father's home and a good mother's counsel, and the society of brothers and sisters; their affections last, while that of such a young man is lost in the wave of the honeymoon.

Chatham [New Brunswick] *Gleaner*, December 7, 1878

Two young Portage ladies took advantage of their leap year privileges the other day and proposed to a young dry goods clerk who works in an Avenue store. He accepted both offers, and then one of the young ladies was cruel enough to say that she was sorry he accepted her offer because she would sooner have a new silk dress than him.

Portage La Prairie Weekly Tribune, February 8, 1884

The Course of True Love - A few days ago, John Mooney, of Erin, cut his foot so badly while chopping wood that he could not leave his bed. To be crippled was bad enough at any time, but what troubled John most was the fact that his wedding day was fixed, and now an indefinite stay in the proceedings loomed up. However, as the Fergus News-Record states, the bride elect, daughter of Mr. and Mrs. John McDonald, a neighboring farmer, was a true-hearted girl, entering into matrimony from the best of all motives, pure and unalloyed affection, and the groom being unable to go to her, she went to him, and the marriage ceremony was performed on Dominion Day, the date arranged, while he lay helpless upon his couch.

Acton Free Press, July 22, 1886

Judging from present signs, the divorce cause list for the next session of the Senate will be heavy. In three cases notice has been given already, and a fourth notice is expected. Three cases come from Western Ontario, and the fourth is from British Columbia. Divorce in Canada is an expensive luxury, each being estimated to cost at least $1,000.

London Advertiser, July 18, 1889

A somewhat romantic marriage took place Sunday at the Roman Catholic church in this village, between Japhet Landriau and Miss Hotte, a young lady of some 23 summers. It appears that Mr. Hotte had refused Landriau's suit, and forbid his daughter from seeing him. During mass, the father being away to church, Landriau drove up to the door and res-

cued the blushing bride, and after driving down another road to the church, they were quietly married. L'Orignal Advocate.
Alexandria Glengarrian, August 30, 1895

There are 3 Winnipeg women in Grand Forks suing for divorces from their husbands. It is needless to say that there are not that many there hunting for wash tubs.
Brandon Mail, March 5, 1896

The wife of a prominent citizen of Little Current has fled with a Church of England catechist, officiating as minister of the Anglican church, where the lady acted as organist.
Smith's Falls Echo, April 1, 1896

A man likes to feel that he is loved, a woman likes to be told.
Cardston Record, September 3, 1898

Chapter Eleven

Piety & Morality

Although they could be fun-loving and passionate, our ancestors largely shaped their world along strict lines of morality and piety. God, Jesus Christ, the Bible, and the church were strong forces in the lives of a great many. To the religious, gambling, swearing, drinking, smoking, sloth and idleness, infidelity, licentiousness, immoral literature, and Sabbath-breaking were intolerable sins that had absolutely no place in their society. With evangelical fervor, and through sermons, revival meetings, public demonstrations, the printed word, statutes, by-laws, and so on, dedicated flocks of Christian soldiers set out to eradicate vice from their midst. Their cherished goal was to purify civilization and thereby pave the way for Christ's millennial return. While few ever openly questioned the word of God, exactly what He intended was the subject of significant social debate. Indeed, journalists of a century ago did not have to look very far for ample evidence that not everyone desired to obey the dominant moral code.

We must decline inserting the advertisement sent us of the horse race at St. Anciet. If reasonable men would only consider that horse-racing is great cruelty to a useful animal, that it encourages idleness and drinking, and is directly promotive of gambling (for what else is betting?), we are sure they would not give it the slightest countenance.

Huntingdon Canadian Gleaner, January 3, 1868

A Clerical Strike - In a neighboring town a few Sunday mornings ago, the congregation were gathered for worship. The minister came in, took his place amongst the members, and showed no signs of intending to officiate. After some delay, some of the members asked him to begin the services, but he refused, saying that if they would not pay him his salary, which they were well able to do, he could not afford to preach. This brought them to terms and the next day arrangements were made to pay up and provide for the future. We recommend the policy to others similarly circumstanced.

Oshawa Vindicator, February 19, 1868

Swearing is an abominable vice which generally goes hand in hand with the use of strong drink. It is a useless, nasty, ungentlemanlike vice, a sin against God, a crime against human law, and an infallible sign of low breeding and bad manners.

Halifax Evening Express, September 4, 1868

An Idle Lot - Any day one may see a lot of able-bodied fellows going about the town with their hands in their pockets, poisoning the air with the smoke of the vilest tobacco, who might all be honestly and profitably employed if they were not too lazy to look for work. And yet they complain of the hardness of the times, and the difficulty of getting anything to do. The fact is, many of our citizens experience great trouble in getting a man to cut a cord of wood, and almost every day applications are made at City Hall for men to do this work. Not long ago, one of these self-same idlers was asked by a gentleman to cut some wood for him, and the gentleman was not a little disgusted to hear the fellow jocularly excuse himself because, as he said, his bucksaw wasn't in tune! Jokers, like this one, who scorn honest labor when it is to be had, are not above sending their barefooted children to the Relief Committee in the cold depths of winter to whine about the scarcity of victuals, or to the post office to beg a penny of everyone who should go in or come out because ma hadn't a bit of bread in the house. Oh, no!

London Free Press, November 13, 1869

Mr. John Chew of the Waverley barber shop has resolved for the future to close his establishment on Sunday. This is very commendable on his part, and we trust that the other knights of the razor will follow the good example which he has set. People who neglect to clean their faces till the Sabbath will hereafter have to seek for John's services in vain on that day.

Stratford Herald, April 16, 1873

The meeting for special prayer tonight will be held in the North Street Wesleyan Church. Subject: "Prayer for nations that peace and righteousness may prevail, that intemperance, vice, infidelity and superstition may be banished."

London Advertiser, January 8, 1874

One of our very fastidious young ladies was greatly shocked the other day in being informed that our friend Wood had male and female strawberries in the same bed. While she was uttering "The nasty thing" we left.

Granby Gazette, May 22, 1874

For playing baseball on Sunday, near London [Ontario], two youths were each fined $1 and costs.

Clinton New Era, August 13, 1874

Clinton News - We learn that a book peddler is endeavoring to sell a small book containing accounts of the Beecher and Clendenning scandals got up in the most sensational style. We would advise our readers not to purchase the trash, as it is unfit for the table of any respectable family. Such works and peddlers are not wanted here.

Mitchell Advocate, September 10, 1875

The ice was thronged with boy skaters yesterday, many of them learners, who with their frequent falls broke the ice as well as the 5th Commandment.

Chatham [Ontario] *Tri-Weekly Planet*, December 30, 1878

Manitowaning has 3 churches and a temperance society. This speaks well for the moral standing of our village.

Manitoulin Expositor [Manitowaning], May 24, 1879

Last evening the Congregational Church in Brantford was thrown into a state of general excitement. On Sunday the 4th of January, the Rev. S.P. Barker resigned his pastorate of the Church, and last evening he preached his farewell sermon to a crowded house. Before commencing his sermon, the Rev. gentleman gave as his reason for resigning that his congregation were guilty of duplicity and meanness towards him, and turning on the choir, he made a rather personal attack on them when some retired. This caused one of the gentlemen in the choir to stand up and request the Rev. gentleman to stop his insult. The Rev. gentleman requested the speaker to sit down, when the gentleman threatened to start the organ and drown his voice. At this stage, a lady in the congregation fainted. The Rev. gentleman continued his attack, and when a number were leaving, he requested them to be seated as the objectionable part of his sermon was over. He then proceeded with his sermon.

Owen Sound Advertiser, January 22, 1880

There is more gambling in town than the letter of the law calls for.

Edmonton Bulletin, January 16, 1883

The bachelors turned out by the barrelful to hear the sermon "Looking for a wife" on Sunday night last.

Embro Courier, September 10, 1884

Sunday Skating - On Sunday afternoon a large number of young men and boys were skating on the river just above the City Hall landing. Some of them who saw Sergeant Vandine approaching were surprised to think he also intended to skate. But when the policeman, after coming out on the ice in the midst of the skaters, drew from his pocket, instead of a pair of skates, a notebook and pencil, and began making notes therein, the skaters were not long in taking the hint. In two minutes there was not a skater to be seen. They left so quickly that the sergeant had not time to get a name down.

Fredericton Evening Capital, November 25, 1884

The subject of debate before the Caledonian Club Literary Society on Monday evening will be: "Is the reading of Novels injurious to Morals?"

Charlottetown Daily Examiner, March 13, 1886

Rev. W. McDonagh, in a sermon at Strathroy recently, characterized horse-racing as affording Satan a better opportunity of exercising his influence on mankind than any other form of iniquity.

Acton Free Press, September 16, 1886

Lecture on Infidelity - The Rev. George Sexton, M.A., D.D., etc. (one of the most accomplished lecturers against the infidelity of the day) will preach in the Main Street Methodist Church on Sunday evening.

Brampton Conservator, April 8, 1887

We are informed that some of the Port Arthur people threaten to have the owners of the ship Kakabeka indicted for running Sunday excursions.

Fort William Journal, September 15, 1887

The landlord of the Callender House in Kingston, objecting to the Salvation Army singing and praying in front of his hotel, turned on the hose and quickly dispersed the crowd.

Bowmanville Canadian Statesman , August 22, 1888

We notice from an exchange that William Reid of Parry Sound is serving 10 days in jail for swearing on the streets. If all the young men who swear on the streets in Gravenhurst were served in the same way, our jail accommodation would require to be considerably enlarged.

Gravenhurst Banner, October 4, 1888

The young ladies of Aylmer, Ontario have organized and pledged themselves not to keep company with any young man who drinks, smokes or plays cards. May such organizations increase and flourish. What do the young ladies of Charlotte-town think of it?

Charlottetown Guardian, March 3, 1891

A "brush-cutting bee" was held on Tuesday evening, when two score of willing hands assisted Rev. Mr. Langrill to clear the lots donated as a site for the Presbyterian Church.

Vernon News, July 2, 1891

There will be fifty-three Sundays in 1893 - a kind of leap year for the contribution boxes.

Millbrook Reporter, January 26, 1893

Messrs. Crossley and Hunter, the evangelists, completed their labors in Port Elgin Sunday this week, the last meeting being attended by nearly 3,000 people. As a result of the services, close on 350 persons professed conversion and their desire to lead a Christian life. These people are distributed among the churches of the town and neighborhood. On Monday morning a large number of people accompanied the evangelists to the station, and as the train moved out, heartily joined in singing "God be with you till we meet again." The visit of Crossley and Hunter to Port Elgin was the occasion of deep and widespread interest, and assisted as they were by the active workers in all the churches, they no doubt accomplished much good. Their stay here will be long remembered. They are now enjoying a few weeks' rest at St. Thomas and Chicago.

Port Elgin Times, August 9, 1893

Mr. John Stewart, son of Mr. William Stewart of Darling, died last week in the Brockville Insane Asylum. Mr. Stewart had been there but 3 or 4 weeks when his end came. He became an invalid through some cerebral malformation that was started or developed, it is thought, by excessive religious excitement. Much sympathy goes out for Mrs. Stewart and children, the wife and family whom the deceased leaves to mourn his loss.

Lanark Era, July 24, 1895

Evangelist Pugsley talked to a full house last evening at the Baptist Church. The address was a trenchant exposure of the folly of neglecting divine counsel. Service continues this week in the Baptist Church at 8 p.m.

Edmonton Bulletin, July 25, 1898

Chapter Twelve

Demon Rum

The temperance movement, perhaps, stands as the most profound manifestation of Victorian moral reform. During the last three-quarters of the nineteenth century, an unyielding army of teetotalers waged a constant crusade to banish strong drink from society. King alcohol had to fall in defeat, because, according to the drys, drunkenness was responsible for more social misery than any other form of iniquity. Despite their strong numbers, prolific sermonizing, and sometimes successful legislative lobbying, warm friends of the temperance cause met persistent opposition from an entrenched, yet less vociferous corps of dedicated participants in Canada's Victorian drink culture. The press captured the essence of both camps in the war over the bottle, and devoted gallons of ink to stories about drunken indulgences, the temperance campaign, the less obnoxious aspects of the drinking world, and defiance of local-option prohibition.

Putting Liquor Through the Bars - About noon on Saturday, Constable Rousseaux detected a man named Wilson supplying some of his female friends with two bottles of "forty rod" through the bars of the King William Street police station cells. He was arrested and locked up.

Hamilton Spectator, February 11, 1867

A Total Abstinence Society was formed on Monday evening at the public meeting held in the Wesleyan Chapel. A considerable number signed the temperance pledge and many more, it is believed, will follow the example shortly.

Sackville Borderer, April 3, 1868

The son of a clergyman was setting a good example last Tuesday night by kicking up a row about town while in a beastly state of intoxication.

Winnipeg Nor'wester, October 24, 1868

Where is our constable? For the last three Sabbaths our town has been disgraced by the appearance of drunken men on the streets, insulting our peaceable citizens, and we have not heard of a single arrest. As the law stands now, these men are punishable for drunkenness, and their evidence can be compelled against those who violate our license law by selling liquor on Sunday.

Trenton Courier, June 9, 1870

An interesting disciple of St. Crispin [a shoemaker], who lately has made Newmarket his local habitation, had a tussle with John Barleycorn last Sunday morning and got "floored." When people were returning from church, he laid stretched out on a piece of timber near Main Street, locked in the arms of Morpheus. These ways won't do.

Newmarket Era, October 21, 1870

A Vicious Practice Revived - We regret to be compelled to say that the doings and experiences of Tuesday show that the system of refreshments for the Electors - which in reality means free liquors - and which has been very generally condemned by the moral sentiment of the County, has been revived in all its perniciousness. The Confederate Party [pro-Confederation] supplied rum in unlimited quantities at every polling booth, the consequences of which in many places were disgraceful to us as a people. We say this altogether apart from political or party considerations. In East Pictou the Anti-Confederate Party supplied no liquors. In West Pictou, we believe, both parties had their open houses. The practice is wrong, injurious to the morality of the people, and the party which persists in maintaining it will find that they have assumed a burden which will soon become too heavy to be borne.

New Glasgow Eastern Chronicle, May 18, 1871

Mr. John McDonald of Arnprior met a sudden death on the evening of Wednesday last by apoplexy supposed to have been induced by intoxicating liquors.

Carleton Place Herald, November 1, 1871

Unpleasant News for Some Folks - Business letters received from the old country by the last mail intimate that there has been a rise in the price of Scotch whiskey.

St. Catharines Weekly News, October 24, 1872

Petitions for presentation to the different legislative bodies, asking for the prohibition of the liquor traffic, are being circulated in various parts of the county and numerously signed.

Picton Gazette, December 20, 1872

A Startling Story for Pictou Rum Drinkers - We are credibly informed that last summer a corpse preserved in liquor was sent home from the United States to a certain place in this County. The man to whose care the corpse was sent, being

somewhat economical in his disposition, and opposed to anything like extravagance, drew the liquor off the corpse and retailed it by the glass to customers who doubtless considered it first rate liquor. Those who got the liquor can reflect over the story at their leisure. - [New Glasgow] Eastern Chronicle.
Halifax Morning Chronicle, January 3, 1874

A Cold Dip - A drunken man-of-war sailor broke a window in a shop on Water Street last night. On being hotly pursued, he ran down Taylor's Wharf and attempted to jump on board a schooner, which being too far off, he fell between the vessel's side and the wharf. He was rescued by his pursuers in an exhausted condition. The shopkeeper declines to prosecute, thinking the sailor has had punishment enough.
Halifax Morning Chronicle, January 16, 1874

The beastly, yet sad exhibition, of a woman drunk and reeling through the streets we are glad to say is a rare occurrence here. On two occasions last week we saw a woman quite intoxicated searching around the town for a yet more drunken husband. It is disgusting enough to see a man worse of liquor, tumbling through the streets and describing to the amusement of a crowd of boys or thoughtless young men all sorts of acrobatic feats, but when a woman so forgets herself, and by such action makes herself the subject of ridicule, of sneer, and of ribaldry, we are horrified.
North Sydney Herald, June 17, 1874

A drunkard's wife in West Oxford horse-whipped the tavern-keeper who supplied her husband with whiskey the other day.
Clinton New Era, August 30, 1874

A schoolmaster from Philipsburg, named Brownlow, who had informed upon a number of hotel-keepers for selling liquor on Sunday, was driven out of New Hamburg on Saturday under a shower of rotten eggs. The authorities were power-less to protect him.

Clinton New Era, April 1, 1875

This afternoon Tax Collector Caven, assisted by officers Detlor and Donaghy, seized an illicit still in the house of one White on the Bayfield road. The still is supposed to have been in operation during the winter. At the time of the seizure, the distillation of one mash had just been completed, and two more were in the process of fermentation. All the apparatus connected with it and also a small quantity of spirits were confiscated.

Mitchell Advocate, May 28, 1875

The meanest man in the country has been found in Galt. On Thursday evening he stole a goose-hollow thermometer for the sake of the alcohol in it. By returning the broken instrument to its owner, he may save the detection to which his large foot prints may lead.

Galt Reformer, February 23, 1876

Mrs. Goff lectured to about 200 persons in the Temperance Hall last night, many of whom signed the temperance pledge and received the blue ribbon. She speaks again this evening at 8 o'clock at the same place.

Moncton Daily Times, August 14, 1877

We are informed that the hotelkeepers are now charging ten cents a drink to all those old topers who voted for the Dunkin [local-option prohibition] by-law. In fact, some of those hotelkeepers refuse to give them liquor on any consideration, being determined to assist them in keeping temperate. Others we hear of have been rather summarily hustled out of the bar-rooms for their inconsistency.

Peterborough Review, November 16, 1877

At a legal investigation of a liquor seizure, the judge asked an unwilling witness: "What was in the barrel you had?" The reply was: "Well your honor, it was marked "whisky" on one end of the barrel and "Pat Duffy" on the other end, so that I can't say whether it was whisky or Pat Duffy that was in the barrel, being as I am on oath."

Carbonear Herald, July 24, 1879

Sault Ste. Marie - A creature calling himself a man left his wife and child on an island in the [St. Mary's] river on Tuesday, while he acted the jolly good fellow and got beastly drunk. Fortunately, the woman was seen and taken off by a passing boat late in the evening.

Manitoulin Expositor [Manitowaning], September 6, 1879

Two drunken railway laborers had a scuffle on the street at Yale on Sunday last. One fell down and the other sat down on him, exclaiming, "You owe me six bits and I'll cut your throat for it!" This he proceeded to do, but being rendered unsteady by whiskey, he merely made two deep cuts on the cheek of his prostrate companion. The wounded man was duly attended to , but lost a great deal of blood. The operator was taken care of in the gaol.

New Westminster Mainland Guardian, September 15, 1880

Those who desire to indulge in enlivening drinks while living in this North-West under the tyrannical rule of a prohibitory law, when the pure quill cannot be obtained take to strange substitutes. Anything that is found to contain alcohol "goes." Pain killer in its various forms, flavoring extracts and essences, all manner of medicinal bitters and wines, and even cologne water are either taken pure or used as the basis of mixtures of more or less deadly qualities to produce the desired exhilaration. The latest discovery, which has been very popular lately, is known by the darkly suggestive nickname of "coffin varnish."

Edmonton Bulletin, March 10, 1883

A young man named John Robinson was found sitting upright on his sleigh on the road between the Portage and Westbourne, Manitoba, on the 31st of January, frozen stiff. A [liquor] jug in the sleigh gave all the explanation necessary.
Edmonton Bulletin, March 17, 1883

The Liquor License Inspectors are taking advantage of every means for the suppression of the sale of liquor in this city. On Saturday evening a consignment of liquor arrived by the five o'clock train. The officers knew it and were on hand at the station to follow the liquor to its destination. It was put on a sloven, but so closely did the officers watch the movements of this wagon, that instead of landing the liquor, the driver was compelled to take his load out of town.
Fredericton Evening Capital, April 22, 1884

The Calgary brewery is next to the Woodbine and manufactures a "hop beer" that reminds us of the "hop" of long ago. It is a pleasant and palatable beverage, which the most eminent blue ribbon [temperance] man may take without prejudice. But if hop beer is a pleasant beverage, the hop porter is really nectar for the gods. It cheers, but does not do the other thing [intoxicate].
Calgary Nor'wester, April 29, 1884

Hiram Walker of Walkerville [now part of Windsor, Ontario] is distilling 5,000 gallons of whiskey a day.
Dutton Enterprise, March 5, 1885

A Wingham correspondent remarks: The Scott Act [local-option prohibition] being in force does not seem to make any difference here. Beer and whiskey are still the popular beverages, and all the topers apparently get their "bitters," as they call them, with usual regularity.
Huron Expositor, May 22, 1885

Mrs. Letitia Youmans, the famous Canadian temperance

lecturer, will deliver a lecture in the Methodist church in this city on the evening of Friday, June 25th.

Nanaimo Free Press, June 19, 1886

One of our prominent temperance advocates has been recommending salts to keep out the cold, as a substitute for liquor when so used. This is doubtless the very latest scientific discovery.

Acadia Mines Week's Doings, December 17, 1886

There are now eight hotelkeepers and one bar boy in the Walkerton jail for refusing to pay Scott Act [local-option prohibition] fines.

Bruce Herald, March 1, 1888

When two women who are friends meet on the street, they smile right there. When two men who are friends meet on the street, they adjourn to the nearest saloon to "smile."

Norwich Gazette, August 9, 1888

A cargo of "irrepressible" was "coralled" on the highway by Constable Doyle this week. Inspector Constantine would not "permit" such spirituous innovations; consequently mother earth absorbed the spirituous fluid. We are of the earth earthy; what's the matter with us absorbing?

Moosomin Courier, April 11, 1889

Temperance Column (Wingham W.C.T.U.) - The reason why some men can't make both ends meet is because they are too busily engaged in making one end drink.

Wingham Times, January 10, 1890

The Prohibitionists are beginning to move in the matter of putting their candidates in the field for the ensuing Dominion elections.

Truro Signal, September 13, 1890

A sorrowful-looking sight on our streets Tuesday was a

mother trying to lead along a young lad about fifteen years of age so drunk that he could scarcely walk.

Sudbury Journal, February 16, 1893

A good story is told about an old lady voter in the recent municipal elections. She could not read or write and she told the returning officer she wanted to vote for Mr.-----. "Very well, madam," said the obliging official as he marked the lady's ballot. He then added, "What about Prohibition?" "I don't know the man at all," said the lady, "and I won't vote for him."

Port Elgin Times, January 10, 1894

If the saloons were as badly lighted as some churches, there wouldn't be so many drunkards.

South Edmonton News, July 23, 1896

There was a wedding feast at Tillsonburg, Ontario on the 8th instant, and Miss Jessie Carruthers was to have been married. Every person had come: clergyman, best man, relatives, and friends. The groom came, too, but he came very drunk. Thereupon the prospective bride announced that the wedding was cancelled and the young man was free. That girl's head was level. A man who showed his prospective bride so little respect as to appear at the altar intoxicated would hardly make a model husband.

Huntsville Forester, July 16, 1897

Chapter Thirteen

That Vilest of Weeds

Tobacco use was another topic that Victorian Canadians debated. In the 1800s, the nicotine habit was almost the exclusive preserve of men. However, much to the dismay of many social commentators, some brash women and children also displayed their penchant for the weed in public. Smokers found their greatest delight in puffing on pipes and cigars, and they enthusiastically filled the air with a smoky haze. (Cigarettes did not really become popular until after the turn of the century.) Still others found satisfaction in a nice chew of tobacco, and they nonchalantly expectorated the tarry residue not just in spittoons, but on floors and all over sidewalks and streets. Of course, not everyone appreciated the pleasures of tobacco. In newspaper columns across the land, the weed was attacked for being a threat to the morality and health of its users, with the most acute shock and disgust often exhibited in reports about youthful smokers. Even so, the other side of the issue - the joy of the habit - also received press coverage, *butt* tellingly to a much lesser extent.

The Anti-Tobacco Society will meet at Pike's School House, 10th Concession, Markham, on Friday evening the 17th instant, at half past seven o'clock, for despatch of business. A general attendance is requested.

Markham Economist, September 16, 1869

A cigar contains acetic, formic, butyric, valeric and proprionic acids, prussic acid, creosote, carbolic acid, ammonia, sulphuretted hydrogen, pyridine, viridine, picoline, and rubidene, to say nothing of cabbagine and burdockic acid. That's why you can't get a good one for less than five cents.

London Free Press, November 25, 1876

Tobacco - Dr. Herriman delivered a very interesting lecture last Friday evening in the Hall of the YMCA. His subject was "Tobacco." The Dr. handled his subject in a very able manner, and showed the deleterious effect the use of the weed had in the system, and the disease and death that was engendered in consequence of its use, as well as the filthy practice in all decent society, and warned the boys present not to use the weed in any form. The lecturer stated the alarming fact that there were no less than thirty-five boys attending the Central School who used tobacco, and no doubt in most cases without the knowledge of their parents. This practice should be stopped.

Port Hope Guide, November 30, 1876

The promising brains of too many young men end in cigar smoke.

London Free Press, April 11, 1877

Springfield has a boy four years old who can smoke two pipes of tobacco in succession.

Ingersoll Chronicle, June 6, 1878

A bill, prohibiting the sale of cigarettes to boys, is before the

New York Legislature. Why not introduce a bill to the same effect in our own legislature? The boy smoker is a nuisance and a reproach to the age. He is to be met everywhere puffing at villainous cigars, and not only making himself a nuisance, but ruining himself both morally and physically.

Huron Signal, February 15, 1884

The smoking concert [party] at the [Mounted Police] barracks this evening will be a very enjoyable affair: the whole of the male population is going.

Calgary Herald, December 10, 1889

We have noticed on several occasions numbers of small boys on the streets smoking away as if their lives depended on their efforts. These boys are not yet in their teens, and such a habit should be discouraged by the vigorous application of the shingle or some compulsory way. There is something more ennobling for a mere boy to do than to be puffing his young manhood away at the end of a pipe.

Buckingham Post, May 16, 1895

Civilization has surely reached an unusual degree in this country. A native of this country, a resident of Moosehide, about 10 years of age, was noticed parading Main Street the other day contentedly puffing a cigarette.

Yukon Sun, March 13, 1900

Chapter Fourteen

Pranksters, Scamps & Delinquents

Adolescent and young adult males have traditionally constituted the most restless and dangerous element in our society. On a less threatening level, pre-pubescent boys have usually made up the most scampish class. The common bond between both age groups has always been their penchant for testing the boundaries of authority. Despite a governing ethic of uprightness and order, nineteenth-century Canada did not escape the shenanigans of young males (and sometimes their elders). Newspapers of the era are filled with reports about the mischievous exploits of boys, including loafing about, setting off firecrackers, pulling fire alarms, skinny dipping, throwing snowballs, playing hookey, and "general skylarking."

Journalists, however, did not stop with simple accounts of such behaviour. Rather, the press usually assumed the role of community watchdog and castigated youngsters for their unruliness, in order to demonstrate that proper decorum was expected. In addition, newspapers, with an eye to warning would-be delinquents, carried reports about the stiff penalties that youths often suffered for their misdeeds. On the other hand, subtle tones of admiration found their way into stories about good-natured, harmless pranks. Even so, juvenile rowdiness, vandalism, and theft met with sharp rebuke, and the identities of the perpetrators of such acts were sometimes broadcast in hopes that community admonition would steer wayward parties back to the straight and narrow.

Boys given to the rascally, unmanly habit of throwing firecrackers about the streets at ladies had better give it up on Monday if they want to dispense with a course of Mr. Payette's bread and water, as the police have received strict orders to arrest all boys who use them, and will be assisted by a large number of extra policemen in plain clothes.

Montreal Gazette, July 1, 1867

We understand that a number of young men in this village are in the habit of prowling around backyards and on top of people's houses when the unconscious inmates are retiring. This is certainly not creditable conduct and we fully believe the parties would not like to see their names in print. Let them desist.

North Middlesex Review, September 6, 1867

The juvenile depravity of Guelph is appalling.

Hamilton Evening Times, August 15, 1868

Police Court - A boy named John O'Laughlans, a Corktown sprout, was charged with throwing manure through the window of Daniel Moran's residence. Fined $1.

Hamilton Evening Times, August 19, 1868

About half-past four on Saturday afternoon some boys rang the Portland Street fire bell for sport, and as a consequence, the fire brigade turned out. This kind of sport must be put to a stop.

Toronto Leader, July 5, 1869

On the night of the 25th of September, the domicile of a lone couple named Fletcher, living a short distance out of the city in London Township, was invaded by a pack of drunken rowdies, between the ages of fifteen and twenty, who abused the inmates in a shocking manner, and turned the place into a little pandemonium. They broke the dishes and furniture without discrimination, and when they left, a sickening scene of ruin and desolation was presented. In this job some half dozen or more scoundrels were engaged, one of whom is said to have been the Frederick Primrose who was arrested by Constable Phair on Saturday night. The case has been remanded for a time, for obvious reasons.

London Free Press, November 9, 1869

The sudden fall of snow on Friday was a great source of amusement to our juveniles, who immensely enjoyed the fun that it afforded of plastering each other with the soft plastic mass, or as opportunity would offer, stealing a random shot at the more sobersided citizens when the policeman's back was turned. These "side issues" the youngsters seemed to regard as the chief enjoyment.

Habour Grace Standard, December 6, 1873

On Saturday last while St. Peter's Church was opened for the nuns to decorate the altar, two lads climbed the paling, and while one of them stood sentinel, the other entered the church and robbed the poor box. They made off with the spoils, which probably amounted to $20, as it was just before the season for opening the box to distribute the Christmas donations to the poor of the congregation. To say nothing of the sacrilegious nature of the act, there could be hardly conceived a meaner theft than such a robbery of the poor.

Peterborough Review, December 28, 1877

Some scamp, operating between Saturday night and Monday morning, defaced the new Domville Building in a scandalous way by daubing the fine corner stones - both free stone and granite - with a large quantity of black ink. The stones will need to be worked over again and about a sixteenth of an inch taken off the stones all around. The author of the outrage, when discovered, should be severely punished.

St. John Daily Sun, August 21, 1878

Sarnia seems to have its share of juvenile rowdies, who loaf around hotel doors and street corners on Sunday evenings and insult ladies on their way home from church. Will the police kindly help us to publish their names.

Sarnia Observer, May 2, 1879

Complaint has been made at the News office that a club of youths hold forth nightly in a shanty on the northern end of Pitt Street, between Leinster and King Streets, which is demoralizing in its tendencies and a discredit to the community. The complaint asks that the attention of the police be directed to the place in question, and to the gambling and other vices which there find encouragement.

St. John Daily News, November 27, 1879

About half a dozen or so boys of all shades of color and nation are in the habit of nightly congregating in front of the fire engine hall, and passing their time in swearing, stone-throwing, and general skylarking - much to the annoyance of residents and passers-by. Cannot an end be put to this nuisance?

New Westminster Mainland Guardian, April 10, 1880

Complaints are being frequently made as to the misconduct of boys while bathing in the river. On several occasions lately, a crowd of nude boys gathered around a pleasure boat and tried to upset it. This cannot be allowed. One or two examples must be made of those who forget themselves so far, and we have no doubt that if the Mayor should be called on to interfere, he will teach them a lesson they will not soon forget.

St. Mary's Argus, July 12, 1881

The people of Stayner see ghosts - real live ones too. A merchant was on his way home one night last week, when he was confronted by a "spectre," but not being of a nervous temperament, he stood his ground until the object made a retreat, when he gave chase and captured it, but failed to identify the party in disguise.

Alliston Weekly Herald, November 10, 1881

Some of those inveterate and unspeakable small boys who make a practice of hanging on passing sleighs will come to grief one of these days. The police should make an example of them before they furnish food for the undertaker.

Brandon Mail, April 7, 1883

During the past week, large numbers of suckers have been caught in the Maitland River by boys, some of whom should probably have been at school. The boys find a more congenial and certainly a much more natural recreation spearing suckers in the open air than studying language within the walls of a school room. The suckers are found in the river this year in larger quantities than usual.

Listowel Banner, May 4, 1883

Some of the scholars in the High School had a good laugh on All Fools' morning at the expense of their teacher and associates. They appear to have gained access to the school in the dark hours of the night and placed on the teacher's table a corpse. The janitress came to the school in the morning to discharge her accustomed duties, but on seeing the corpse labeled "Small Pox," she refused to go near it, and the scholars on coming to school also fought shy of it. The principal next came, and walking up to it cautiously, lifted the sheet and saw on the corpse the inscription in not very small letters, "April Fool." It was a pretty cleverly devised trick of the boys and has created a good deal of amusement. The corpse on being dissected proved to be a suit of clothes stuffed with old papers, having on the feet a pair of slippers and on the head a white hat. It looked very natural with the toes turned up and the body covered with a snow white sheet of paper on which was hanging a board of health placard, "Small Pox," with a skull and crossbones on top and a hearse underneath. A flag still floats from the eave of one of the gables of the school with a skull and crossbones painted on it, which the same practical jokers placed there. Keep quiet boys - the teacher is after you.

Sarnia Observer, April 3, 1885

A couple of boys amused themselves on Tuesday by firing a broadside of revolver bullets through the public school windows. Thirty-nine panes were fractured. A whitewasher working in the building at the time was badly scared. It is reported that the son of a local citizen and a city chum who was visiting with him played the contemptible trick. The youth's friends will repair the damage done.

Acton Free Press, August 5, 1886

A farmer who bought binding twine at Oakville last week was the victim of the bad boys of that village. They noticed the end of a ball hanging out of the wagon and hitched on immediately, and the farmer, not noticing the trick, drove on, and soon five or six hundred yards of twine were laid up the street. The sentiments expressed by the farmer on discovering his loss are not recorded, but they were expressive enough.

Acton Free Press, August 5, 1886

Some of the Halloween practical jokers made house-breakers of themselves on Saturday night and cut the rope of the public school bell all to pieces, besides other depredations.

Acton Free Press, November 4, 1886

The police should be on the alert to put down the firecracker nuisance. A public notice will help to diminish the evil.

Lindsay Canadian Post, May 20, 1887

On Monday night Mr. J. Scully retired to bed, leaving two easy chairs standing on the verandah at his house. Next morning the chairs were missing. Mr. Scully searched the neighborhood and gave it up. On Wednesday night the chairs were placed back exactly as Mr. S. left them. No reward is offered for information that will lead to the conviction of the innocent party or parties.

Lindsay Canadian Post, June 3, 1887

Some scoundrel plugged a stick of cordwood with an [explosive] cartridge at A.B. Remey's jewelry store last night, and when the stick was placed in the stove this morning, the cartridge exploded, blowing stove lids and doors in sundry directions and doing considerable damage. The police have been notified.

St. Thomas Daily Times, November 25, 1887

Look out now boys, Peter Robertson has been appointed constable and is waiting for the first time any of you are bad. He will clap the "darnies" on and run you into the "caliboose."

Prince Albert Times, September 21, 1888

The breaking of a window pane in the Arkwright post office on Saturday caused a large group of boys to scatter more quickly than chain lightning.

Port Elgin Times, July 5, 1893

The evil resulting from children being on the streets at late hours is attracting the attention of the authorities in many of our towns at present. We notice that Mount Forest has just adopted a curfew regulation. It provides that the school bell be used as the curfew signal, and that the age of children under the operation of the law be all those up to 14 years of age. The bell will be rung ten minutes before the proper time as a warning. The hours at which children are to be off the street are as follows: April, May, June, July and August at 9 o'clock; September and October at 8:30; and for the other months at eight o'clock. Any child found on the streets after these hours without proper guardianship or proper authority shall be warned to go home by the chief constable, who is to see to ringing the bell; and failing to comply, the child is to be escorted home by the chief and the parents notified that the first offence thereafter is punishable by a fine of $1, second offence by $3, third and every subsequent offence by $5.

Parkhill Gazette-Review, September 21, 1893

The snowballing season has set in. Boys who pelt old men, women, or strangers, or who put stones or chunks of ice in snowballs grow up to be bad men, and finally die a miserable death in parliament or some other bad place.

Knowlton News & Brome City Advocate, December 14, 1894

Some boys, who think they excel in cuteness, put cayenne pepper on the stoves in the church one Sunday lately, but were found out before any serious effects were sustained therefrom. We are sorry little boys like those are not kept at home with their "ma's."

Chesterville Record, March 27, 1895

Beaver Hill News - The naughty boys who tied the tin pan to a dog's tail here should be severely punished.

South Edmonton News, June 3, 1895

Cowansville News - On the evening of Wednesday, September 30th, a number of windows in this town were rotten-egged. The guilty ones must remember that such acts are not practical jokes, but are crimes.

Granby Mail, October 3, 1896

Complaints are being made that boys and young men hang around the post office in the forenoon and evening, smoking, swearing, expectorating, etc., and generally making the lobby unpleasant to those getting their mail.

Sherbrooke Daily Record, March 19, 1897

A mid-day sleeper at the Vendome Hotel was rather rudely awakened at noon today. The mid-day sleeper was enjoying a quiet snooze in a chair at the front entrance to the hotel when some wag lighted a huge firecracker and deposited it under the sleeper's chair. The report which followed was a terrific one and the sleeper was unceremoniously aroused from his slumbers.

Sarnia Observer, October 6, 1897

Some unprincipled person has plucked a number of tail feathers from Mr. Ott's peacock. The offender should be severely dealt with if found.

Port Colborne Herald, March 10, 1898

Chapter Fifteen

Law & Order, Crime & Punishment

As previously mentioned, Canadians of a century ago had a keenly developed sense of order. Authority, in all its forms, was to be obeyed above all else. Not so surprisingly, perhaps, our forebears considered crime to be the greatest threat to social harmony. It would appear from their print media that they, just like us, felt as though they were under siege from a swarming army of lawbreakers that counted among its ranks counterfeiters, absconders, short-changers, confidence artists, prostitutes, robbers, pickpockets, home-invaders, brawlers, ruffians, wife-beaters, rapists, and murderers. Although violent crime received the most sensational ink, theft captured the most press attention. Indeed, Victorian thieves stole just about anything they could get their hands on, including town bells, laundry hanging on clotheslines, milk directly from its bovine source, and human cadavers.

Journalists also made a point of conveying news about the administration of law and the execution of punishment, including that meted out by private citizens and in schools. In this regard, it seems that scribes wanted to reassure the public that justice was being done and that good was ultimately triumphing over evil. Of course, subsequent reports about crime, especially that of a violent nature, only served to rekindle community anxiety about the darker elements of their world.

Doors of Public Buildings - Church officials and others should remember that the law directing that doors of public buildings should open outwards goes into effect on the 25th of August. On and after that day, they will be subjected to a fine of $50 if the law has not been complied with.

Belleville Intelligencer, July 22, 1867

Those who were present at the Police court this morning and saw the two young girls, Kearney and Fudge, examined as witnesses to the disorderly character of a house on Barrack Street will be glad to learn, for the sake of morality, that the girls have since been taken care of. The girl Kearney has been sent to the Rev. Foster Almon's "Home for Erring Females," and His Grace the Archbishop of Halifax has kindly offered to take charge of Fudge.

Halifax Acadian Recorder, January 11, 1868

The telegraph lines near the head of Margaret's Bay were cut on Monday last and fifty yards of wire were stolen.

Unionist & Halifax Journal, February 14, 1868

A well known character named Robert Alexander, 3rd Concession, North Georgetown, met with rough usage at the hands of one of the notorious family of Tassies. It appears that Alexander was lying asleep, under the influence of drink, when the Tassie in question poured a quantity of high wines over his face and then set fire to it with a match. The unfortunate man was severely burned in consequence, though we understand not dangerously. Mr. J. Symons, J.P., was to investigate the case on Wednesday, when Tassie would probably be committed for trial.

Huntingdon Canadian Gleaner, May 8, 1868

In the case of Alexander, Mr. Symons, J.P., sentenced Thomas Tassie, Sr., to pay a fine of $20 or go to jail. The fine was paid. The other parties accused were let off.

Huntingdon Canadian Gleaner, June 12, 1868

Beware - After the visit of every circus there is an increase of bogus silver in circulation. Burglaries are also more rife when circuses come around. Let our readers, therefore, be on their guard at the present time. We see by our exchanges that burglaries are becoming more numerous, and safes are being blown open in some city, town or village every night. Constables ought to be on the watch for suspicious characters; we especially advise them to be so in Brockville just now.

Brockville Recorder, August 13, 1868

A parrot was called as a witness in a London [Ontario] Police Court, and its evidence was taken and decided the case.

Hamilton Evening Times, August 17, 1868

Complaints are constantly being made about the large number of boards which are stolen nightly from the sidewalks in various parts of the city.

Hamilton Evening Times, August 20, 1868

The Elora Express says: "Levi J. North's show exhibited in Arthur on Monday last. The people were dissatisfied with the performance, and a row occurred, during which one of the circus men was stabbed and a number of others were more or less injured. Clark's hotel was nearly demolished - the tables were turned over and the were dishes broken up. Such a fight has not been witnessed in Arthur for years."

London Free Press, August 30, 1869

Theft - Two windows were stolen out of the brick building, which is now undergoing repair and belongs to Mr. R. Bishop on Rae Street.

Victoria British Columbian, March 21, 1869

The Chain-Gang - This body, which has in former times presented quite an imposing array of strength and muscle, has dwindled down to a puny squad of four, the solitary and solemn appearance of whom, as they pass in and out of their prison gate and through the streets of the city under the escort of nearly an equal number of armed guards, strongly suggests the possibility of the time having arrived when such an institution might be dispensed with in this colony.

Victoria British Columbian, March 28, 1869

On Thursday night or Friday morning last, some persons entered the Elora Falls Distillery and carried away about 200 gallons of high-wines. The robbers effected an entrance through a small back door and from thence they went into the receiving room. The liquor was in the receiver, and it is supposed they filled it into barrels and carried it away. No clue has yet been obtained as to who the thieves are. Mr. Frazer offers a reward of $200 for the discovery and conviction of the guilty parties.

Fergus News-Record, April 2, 1869

Pickpockets - We are informed that a gang of these nefarious scoundrels were plying their avocation at the entrance of the Music Hall last night and succeeded in abstracting four valuable watches from the pockets of four gentlemen who were forcing their way into the Hall. One of these watches, it is said, was worth $150. Look out for pickpockets!

London Free Press, September 23, 1869

Look out for bogus five dollar bills on the Bank of Montreal. Photographed copies have been circulated in Ontario.

Newcastle Union Advocate, May 11, 1871

Police Court - Ann Agnew has been calling Edward Taylor all manner of obnoxious names, for which she was fined $1 or one week in jail.

Toronto Daily Telegraph, July 6, 1871

Police Court - Mr. Harman, charged by the City Commissioner with having allowed ten geese to run at large on the 10th instant, was fined $1 and costs.

Toronto Mail, July 18, 1873

Some sneak thieves, having a "sweet tooth," entered the premises of Mr. Alexander Gordon, near Bennington, on the night of the 5th instant, and carried off several boxes of honey - containing in all about 24 lbs.

Woodstock Sentinel, August 14, 1874

About three o'clock on Sunday morning last, three masked men entered the house of Mr. Charles Mitchell, near Lakeside, bound Mr. Mitchell and his daughter, ransacked the house, and succeeded in carrying off over $1,000 in cash. The deed was a most daring one and has caused great excitement. There is no clue to the robbers' identities.

Mitchell Advocate, April 9, 1875

Residents of Dartmouth are suffering greatly from an affliction of garden robberies. On Wednesday night, the gardens of Messrs. William, Austen and Henry Elliott were visited by depredators who carried off large numbers of squash and pumpkins, some fine citron, and large quantities of vegetables. There is no clue to the thieves' identities.

Halifax Citizen, October 22, 1875

It is rumoured that the two individuals in town who are in the habit of periodically threshing and otherwise maltreating the "wives of their bosoms" are to be taken out, tarred and feathered and palanquined on a rail - with all that the prosecution of these imposing ceremonies implies - so soon as the weather becomes sufficiently moderate to favor their survival of the treatment. The agitators of the enterprise say that this Great [East] Indian Remedy has never been known to fail of cure even in the most obstinate cases.

Almonte Gazette, December 10, 1875

A Plucky Woman - On the northeast corner of Robert and Catharine streets is situated a house of ill fame. On Saturday evening a married man, well known and respected in this city, was seen going in. The news was conveyed to his wife who came down with a revolver and stood quietly awaiting his coming out. He not being in a hurry, she commenced pelting the door with stones and finally threatened to fire through the window. In the meantime, the man had been let out by a back door and succeeded in escaping. The lady being informed of this, returned home, there to "raise Cain" with her lord and master on his return.

Hamilton Spectator, June 5, 1876

The men who mutinied on board the ship Don Nichols were tried on Tuesday last at Esquimalt. The charge was proved against them, but the captain said he would not prosecute if they would leave the vessel. This the men agreed to do.

Victoria British Colonist, March 29, 1877

Another Den of Infamy - The residents of Augusta Street complain that a woman of ill repute has succeeded in renting a house on that street. The residents would like the police to take up the matter.

Ottawa Citizen, November 13, 1877

Thomas Harcourt, who bit Terrance O'Neil's ear off in a row at Broderick's Hotel at Arthur lately, has been committed for trial.

Orangeville Sun, March 28, 1878

The "Cat o' Nine Tails" was administered to Baker, the London ruffian, last week. Whipping in cases of indecent assault will serve as a punishment where imprisonment would prove unavailing. Let us keep the "cat" by all means.

Ingersoll Chronicle, April 18, 1878

On Thursday last a notorious horse thief named Dechamps, who has long been wanted by the authorities, was brought in by some of the Mounted Police returning from the Sounding Lake payment. An ineffectual attempt to effect his arrest was made some time ago, but he is now in safekeeping at the police quarters across the river.

Saskatchewan Herald, August 26, 1878

Chinaway, also known as Dechamps, left for Manitoba penitentiary on the 9th in custody of Sergeant DeForge.

Saskatchewan Herald, September 23, 1878

Counterfeit half dollars are in circulation.

Chatham [Ontario] *Tri-Weekly Planet*, November 18, 1878

The detectives who arrested the Beverly robbers did a cute thing. They first got the confessions of two of the gang, kept mum until they got the County Council to offer a reward, and then showed their hand.

Brantford Daily Expositor, December 13, 1878

The cigar factory of A. Fair, East Ward, was broken into last night and 5,000 cigars were stolen.

Brantford Daily Expositor, January 8, 1879

It is stated that some loose characters have taken possession of an old schooner anchored in the bay and that it has become a favorite rendevous for young men in the evenings.

Sarnia Observer, June 13, 1879

The floating bawdy house which we mentioned last week set sail for Mooretown the other day. Is there no law able to reach this pestilential old craft?

Sarnia Observer, June 20, 1879

In the Police Court yesterday, four men, George, James, and

William King, and Joseph Butt, were each fined $10 for having fished for salmon with nets on the Pond at Salmon Cove contrary to law.

Carbonear Herald, July 24, 1879

Who Stole the Bell? - During Wednesday night some persons had the audacity to steal and carry off the Town Bell, which had been removed from the old cupola to the sidewalk in front of Dodds' store, previous to being swung in the new tower built for the purpose. The bell is now missing and Council is in a dilemma as to what should be done. If the bell were worth it, we would suggest offering a reward for its recovery through the local paper, and that is sure to fetch it. But our citizens have little regret for their loss and would prefer the expense of getting a new bell for the handsome tower now nearly completed.

Watford Guide-News, September 25, 1879

Ordered to Move On - A professional gambler arrived in our city and thought to spread his nets for unwary celebrants of the Queen's Birthday. He had netted a few pigeons, but before he had squeezed anything out of them Officer Lawrence helped him into the street with all his implements. This is not a good field for such pursuits.

New Westminster Mainland Guardian, May 26, 1880

Our lock-up must be a terror to evil doers, as it has had no patronage since its erection - not even a single "drunk." So might it be.

Lucknow Sentinel, August 26, 1881

Some sneak-thief visited the potato field belonging to Mr. John B. Hicks, 2nd line, Plympton Township, about three weeks ago, and stole from 15 to 20 bushels of valuable potatoes, as well as some extra large pumpkins.

Sarnia Observer, November 4, 1881

A Mrs. Vandermee, wife of a Belgian restaurateur of this city, having lately chosen to enforce certain animadversions of hers upon the conduct of her servant girl, Adeline Michaud, with the more telling argument of the fist, was this morning fined $5 and costs by His Honor the Recorder as a lesson to confine herself in the future to the natural weapon of female argument.

Montreal Star, January 13, 1882

Three members of the Mounted Police have deserted, one of whom was stationed here under Sergeant Bliss. They have gone to Uncle Sam's dominions.

Regina Leader, March 22, 1883

Squire Martin inflicted another fine of "one dollar and costs" last week. It is rumored that a large amount is staked on a bet that the Squire will not raise his fines during 1883 to a sum greater than "one dollar and costs." The accused in the case was an old offender and a chronic nuisance, but all the same the fine was "one dollar and costs."

Wallaceburg Valley Record, April 5, 1883

For the past two months there has not been a case brought before the Magistrate's Court. This is anomalous in the history of the town. Some may attribute it to the wise laws made by the Mowat Administration, others to the naturally law-abiding character of the people in this vicinity, but the more probable cause is the experience past offenders have acquired in Court since the appointment of Justice Draper. There is nothing so powerful to prevent wrong-doing amongst the wrong-doing classes as the full extent of the law being enforced in every case against offenders.

Listowel Banner, April 20, 1883

RUNNING THE GAMUT - The last batch of school teachers sent out from Huron model schools had some strange fellows in it. One of these tyros, who teaches in a northern township, has been giving his experiences to a fellow teacher, and his practice with the "rod" shows that he has a dash of the old time "master" in his composition. He first attempted to enforce authority by the aid of the ruler, next he tried a walking stick, then a birch, followed by the belting of a thrashing machine. This latter instrument of punishment gave way to a pair of taws, but the latest weapon of his pedagogic warfare is a rawhide. We count that a lively three weeks' experience.

Huron Signal, February 8, 1884

The Forest Free Press informs us that "C. Reeves, formerly of Goderich and Clinton, who has been living about here a year, skipped out one night this week, leaving a lot of bad debts behind. He was one of those easy going, shiftless chaps who are of no use to any place. Good-bye Charlie." Reeves put the same dodge over some of his creditors in this town.

Huron Signal, February 15, 1884

A correspondent to the Neepawa Canadian tells of a man in the west who manages to get 2 gallons of coal oil into a 7 quart jug. The inspector of weights and measures, Mr. Bowman, will probably call some of these days to see how this coal oil tick is accomplished.

Portage La Prairie Weekly Tribune, March 7, 1884

The clothesline thieves were around last week, as some of our neighbors found out. Load up your shotguns and get a "dawg."

Stanstead Journal, May 29, 1884

They Must Go! - The corner mugwumps and swigswogs require the constant attention of the police. Queen Street should be systematically patrolled by both of the night officers every evening. The apostles Paul and Zebedee must not weary in well doing, or in other words, they must not let up on 'em. Sergeant Vandine now patrols Queen Street frequently during the daytime and the atmosphere at the corners is now purer. Only stray greenhorns from the bush are now occasionally seen on the corners. The young street Arabs quiz them with the query, "Have you any gum?" These fellows appear to have no means of support, except supporting the corners.

Fredericton Evening Capital, April 19, 1884

A young sport dressed himself in lady's clothes a few nights ago and paraded the back streets to see if he could catch the man who is said to have assaulted numerous ladies. A couple of young fellows who heard that he intended going followed him and the result was a fracas amongst the three. The first mentioned succeeded in capturing a boot belonging to one of the latter two. So far, the boot has not been applied for.

Prescott Telegraph, November 13, 1885

About one thousand feet of lumber that was piled near one of the churches in town was recently stolen. It is mean enough to steal from a private individual, but when it comes down to church property, it is simply contemptible. It seems, however, that the guilty party is likely to be brought to justice. Sufficient clue has been obtained to warrant an arrest and conviction. In a new country, people are compelled for want of accommodation to expose their property publicly, and as a general thing they run very little risk - such is the honesty of the pioneer - but occasionally a being erected upon two legs, bearing all the outward resemblance of a man, finds his way into a new country, and almost immediately that sense of security which hitherto existed, gives place to suspicion and distrust. It becomes a public benediction when characters of that kind are captured and placed in such circumstances as will lead them to a higher sense of right and to enlarged views as to the moral end of man's existence.

Qu'Appelle Progress, November 27, 1885

Charles Dickens, son of the famous novelist, has resigned his commission with the Northwest Mounted Police.

Charlottetown Daily Examiner, March 13, 1886

Orangeville's tax collector has gone to visit Uncle Sam. His collections are $445.99 short.

Acton Free Press, June 3, 1886

The clothesline thief has reached Morden. A few nights ago a quantity of clothing was stolen from a Ninth Street clothesline. It is hoped the thief will be discovered.

Morden Monitor, May 5, 1887

The latest ruse by counterfeiters is to make dollar pieces of glass and cover them with Babbitt's metal. As the spurious coins have a genuine metallic ring, they are difficult to detect.

Mount Forest Representative, July 28, 1887

We are informed that a number of cows in the neighbourhood have been robbed of their milk while feeding in the woods. A "spotter" is on the trail and will make it warm for the guilty party if caught.

Fort William Journal, August 18, 1887

A young woman in male attire paraded St. Catharine Street last evening. This sort of masquerading is becoming quite common and the police should make an example of one or two of the parties.

St. Thomas Daily Times, November 15, 1887

Our attention has been called to a certain country man who has been using unlawful weights in selling fish, etc. around our town. If such a thing is to be continued, we trust the proper officials will look after the matter sharply. Sell as cheaply as you like, but give us honest weight.

Londonderry Times, May 12, 1888

There was not an arrest in Calgary on Christmas Day, or on account of seasonal rejoicing. There have been no arrests for breaches of the peace in Calgary since December 5 - a pretty good showing for a frontier town.

Calgary Herald, December 27, 1889

A chicken thief has been clearing out the hen coops in town during the past week. He is reported to have carried off thirty birds from one place one night last week.

Medicine Hat Times, February 6, 1890

One of the north-end tobacconists has been mulcted in the sum of $50, a fine imposed by the Inland Revenue Department for selling contraband goods brought into the city from the U.S. by one of the porters of the Great Northern Railway. The latter heard the authorities were after him and he remained across the line, corresponding with the department to settle the matter. For the privilege of coming into Winnipeg without fear of arrest, he paid the Dominion government $100.

Winnipeg Daily Tribune, August 7, 1890

McLean, the cross-eyed man who figured in an elopement case with a Mrs. Arnold, and who was arrested here, has been sentenced to seven years in the penitentiary.

Regina Standard, April 24, 1891

The new criminal code, passed at the recent session of the Dominion Parliament, comes into effect today.

Windsor Evening Record, July 1, 1893

A Lindsay butcher was fined $10 and costs, over $30 in all, for exposing for sale diseased meat. The beast was affected with what is known as "lumpy jaw."

Orillia Times, January 4, 1894

The schooner Yucatan was boarded on Monday night by unknown parties and a quantity of beef was stolen. The cabin of the schooner Vivian was also broken into and two or three hundred oranges were stolen.

Lunenburg Argus, April 4, 1894

Presumably taking advantage of the floods, burglars stole the safe of the Moodyville Mills. Their intention evidently was to convey it in a boat to the woods and blow it open. But in shipping it, they managed to let it fall into the water, where it was afterwards found undamaged.

Nelson Miner, June 9, 1894

What appeared at first to be a cannon ball was found the other day on the farm of Mr. Boxall at Surrey Centre. The ball was in two pieces, and on examination there had evidently been a hole through the centre of it. The probable explanation is that some escaped prisoner had there relieved himself of a ball and chain.

Surrey Times, April 12, 1895

A couple of plot owners complain of flowers and plants being stolen from the graves in Camp Hill cemetery.

Halifax Herald, July 3, 1895

A vault in the Roman Catholic cemetery at Kingston was broken into on Saturday night and two bodies were carried off. There is no clue to the perpetrators' identities, but medical students are suspected.

Meaford Monitor, November 8, 1895

The city police should prepare for the gang of swindlers reported to be accompanying the two circuses which are to appear shortly in the city.

Winnipeg Free Press, July 4, 1896

The Chief of Police sent out of the city yesterday a fortune teller and a band of gypsies who were located near the water-works. The latter steered for Toronto and the former for Stratford.

Guelph Daily Mercury, July 16, 1896

Mrs. William Holmes of Barrie was arrested in Barrie for masquerading on the streets in men's clothing. The judge dismissed the charge because the Criminal Code makes no reference to women adopting the garb of men.

Midland Free Press, September 2, 1897

Ben Parrott, the Hamilton murderer, has been declared perfectly sane. He is doubtless sane enough to stretch a rope satisfactorily.

Petrolia Advertiser, June 2, 1899

William Wallace, a farmer living a short distance from Renfrew, was flim-flammed out of $400 by sharpers the other day. It was the old card racket slightly changed. A stranger came along wanting to buy a farm as usual. He was followed by a pal who introduced a game of card drawing. The farmer won $5 and he got anxious. Then he won $4,000 and he was almost tickled to death. But in order to get his last winnings, he had to put $400 in a tin box along with the $4,000. He was given the box to keep till the next day. He became overjoyed in relating his luck to his wife, but she said he was an old fool, and she was right, for when he opened the box, he found that it contained nothing but brown paper.

Merrickville Star, June 29, 1899

Gamblers to the number of 62 were arraigned and paid the usual fine of $10 each.

Yukon Sun, February 13, 1900

Chapter Sixteen

Transportation & Technology

The nineteenth century was an era of great technological innovation. As inhabitants of a vast expanse of land, Victorian Canadians, not so surprisingly, heralded those mechanical advancements that promised to shrink both time and space. Indeed, even though they relied more heavily upon horse-drawn vehicles, our ancestors invariably connected progress, the watchword of their time, with steam engines, railways, the telegraph, and the telephone. They also marvelled at a host of other inventions, ranging from photography to reliable and safe balloon travel. Of course, just as these technologies ultimately changed the world for the better, the press was quick to remind the public that the wonders of the age came with all sorts of new problems and inconveniences. Indeed, even to this day, we still complain that the trains never seem to run on schedule!

ACCIDENT ON THE GRAND TRUNK - Yesterday, as the express was coming up, when it was two miles and a half east of Napanee, a cow jumped on the track just in front of the engine, throwing the engine, baggage, and second class car down the embankment. Fortunately no one was hurt. The driver, D. Preston, stuck to his post till the engine was brought to a stand-still.

Belleville Intelligencer, July 15, 1867

THE PAPER AGE - This is certainly the age of paper. There are "greenbacks," "stamps," paper shirt bosoms, collars and cuffs, paper slippers and hats, paper water pipes, well-walls, and ship cabin panels. Even the sides of pleasure yachts are made of this seemingly fragile material. The latest adaptation of paper, however, comes from Maine, and is specially addressed to the ladies. It is hoped there may be no indelicacy in a simple mention of this new manufacture, which is announced in the local papers as the product of a "Paper Pantalette [underpants] Company." What next?

Unionist & Halifax Journal, February 12, 1868

QUICK PASSAGE - The barque "Royal Alfred," owned by P.W. Hyndman, Esq., of Charlottetown, P.E.I., arrived at Waterford [Ireland] in 14 days from Canso [Nova Scotia]. She had a cargo of oats from Charlottetown. A passage across the Atlantic by sailing vessel in 14 days, at this season of the year, is a good performance.

Halifax Novascotian, January 25, 1869

On Monday the Milton and Bronte stage coach had an upset near Palmero, caused by the breaking of an axle. The passengers, of whom there were eleven, had a lively time before they could regain their perpendicular. Nobody was hurt.

Milton Canadian Champion, May 5, 1870

Photography, like many other discoveries of the present age, is making rapid progress. Mr. Reid, whose gallery is located over the store of Messrs. Orr, is now prepared to execute life-size portraits, as well as the ordinary kinds and sizes.

Newmarket Era, June 3, 1870

The first exportation of hay direct from this city to the United States was made on Wednesday last by train to Bangor. We regret to learn, however, that when the train had reached the Yoho, the hay was discovered on fire, communicated no doubt from the smoke stack of the locomotive, and that with the exception of a few bundles, the whole carload, consisting of ten tons, was entirely destroyed.

Fredericton Colonial Farmer, January 1, 1872

Canada and Australia, 17,000 miles apart, are now within almost instantaneous communication by telegraph. This is a great modern wonder.

St. Catharines Weekly News, November 28, 1872

We notice by telegraph today that the new French telegraph cable is to be landed at Hearts Content, the Halifax terminus having been abandoned, although its shore end was laid a short time since. This is pretty good evidence of the value of Newfoundland as a cable terminus, and this value is certainly not one that should be lightly esteemed either by our government or people.

St. John's Morning Chronicle, May 9, 1873

The sad wrecking of the barque Rivoli lately at Cape Ray was fortunately attended without any loss of life, owing to the daring and hardihood of the fishermen of the neighbourhood, even with the slight means of help at their disposal. Could not a lifeboat or some life-saving apparatus be located in that vicinity - the scene of so much maritime disaster in the past?

Harbour Grace Standard, October 11, 1873

A steam[-powered] man has been invented by C.C. Rowe of Hamilton, and he has it on exhibition in that city. The figure is five feet in height and walks as naturally as a living man. He is capable of walking from four to ten miles an hour. As the owner intends exhibiting his handiwork throughout the Dominion, we may expect to see the curiosity at Waterford.

Waterford Express, July 17, 1874

Tuesday next, August 4th, is the day fixed for Prof. Wise's Balloon Ascension at Stratford, between 3 and 4 o'clock p.m. Tickets of admission to the grounds, 25 cents. The Grand Trunk will carry passengers there and back - tickets are good from the 1st to the 8th instant and are at one and a third fare.

Woodstock Sentinel, July 31, 1874

The telephone will soon revolutionize domestic affairs, for the man, instead of blushingly telling his wife at the tea table that he will be detained at his office, can go down to the city and whisper through the telephone that it is lodge night.

London Free Press, April 12, 1877

S. Hayward & Co. have received a carload of clocks from Hamilton. If that train did not arrive on time, it was not the fault of the freight. There were 2,000 clocks in the car.

St. John Daily Sun, August 3, 1878

A few nights ago, direct telegraphic communication was had between Battleford and Thunder Bay - a distance of twelve hundred miles. The operator at the Bay, however, would not believe it, although he got a lot of Battleford news. He thought some of his friends near at hand were trying to put a joke upon him, and to convince his correspondent that he was not to be taken in, he closed by saying, "Why, Battleford is away out near the Rocky Mountains."

Saskatchewan Herald, February 24, 1879

A few days ago, as the regular stage was proceeding from Collingwood to Owen Sound, it stopped at a hotel on the route. All the male passengers and the driver went into the hotel, leaving Miss J. McLaren, of Paisley, the sole occupant of the stage. The horses, becoming frightened, started off towards Owen Sound at a mad gallop. Miss McLaren was seen by those at the hotel to open the door of the stage, a covered one, and deliberately step out on the rave of the sleigh. This furnished very insecure footing, being only about one and a half inches wide, but by clinging with one hand to the cover of the stage, she managed to steady herself. It was supposed she was watching for a favorable place to jump, but to the astonishment and admiration of the spectators, she was seen to work her dangerous way along the side of the stage till she arrived opposite the driver's seat. Into this she managed to climb and, grasping the reins, brought the madly plunging horses to a stand. By her cool and courageous action, Miss McLaren saved in all probability her own life and several hundreds of dollars to the stage company as well.

Owen Sound Advertiser, January 29, 1880

The railway is about completed to Ayton, twenty-eight miles from Tara. There was great rejoicing on the arrival of the iron horse there last Monday, and reports say beer flowed as freely as water.

Tara Leader, July 7, 1881

THE HARBOR - The Advertiser, of Owen Sound, is laboring under one of its periodic attacks of Collingwood-on-the-brain and makes a few ghastly jokes in reference to our harbor and dry-dock. Of course, Collingwood can stand all that, but it does seem to be the height of absurdity for a mud hole like Owen Sound to be continually puffing its sandbar channel over our safe and commodious harbor.

Collingwood Enterprise, July 6, 1882

Mr. Josiah Doxtator and others have invented a perpetual motion machine. They claim that neither water, steam, wind, nor springs are required. The Oneida are very proud of this invention by these members of their tribe. They also have invented a railway self-switcher, which will be patented this week. We are anxious to see it.

Hagersville Indian, March 17, 1886

The Cornwall telephone exchange now operates forty-two telephones.

Cornwall Standard, March 3, 1887

A span of horses attached to a wagon made a lively exit from town yesterday. The owner arrived on the scene in time to see the contents of his wagon spilled along the road and his spirited steeds disappearing from his view.

Chilliwack Progress, April 30, 1891

For mud and roughness, the road between Rat Portage [now Kenora] and Keewatin takes the cake.

Kenora News, April 20, 1894

It is with much pleasure that we can assure our readers that our town is not wanting in inventive genius. One of our local merchants is the proud employer of a young and promising clerk who is about to patent a potato masher, not to say anything about hat racks.

Qu'Appelle Vidette, January 31, 1895

A drive over the country roads at the present time reminds one somewhat of a rough sea voyage.

St. Mary's Journal, March 7, 1895

Hampton Notes - There was a little improvement in business during the past week, owing to the improvement in the roads.

King's County News, April 25, 1895

Chapter Seventeen

The Rough Waters of Canadian Journalism

Newspaper publishers of a century ago routinely devoted a certain measure of column space to wage verbal war against two determined foes - journalistic competitors and delinquent subscribers. As mentioned in the preamble to the first chapter, the nineteenth century was the age of the political organ. Cities, towns, and many villages were home to at least two newspapers, one Liberal and one Conservative. As one might expect, this circumstance made for some interesting battles in ink. Across the land, editors spared few words in their campaigns against political opponents. Their invectives were often cloaked in humour, but could also be fairly harsh, or even quite libellous. Sincere compliments were only paid to like-minded publishers.

Those in default of their subscription payments were the other bane of the Victorian editor's existence. While hurling volleys at the competition hardly affected the bottom line, delinquent subscribers did. For this reason, publishers were forever pursuing those in arrears. However, since insults were unlikely to encourage people to reach down into their pockets, editors usually resorted to jocularity to get the point across. In addition, journalists employed their columns to remind merchants of the need to advertise and to tender apologies to their readers for late issues, typographical mistakes, and refusals to print unsolicited submissions.

If the Halifax Chronicle critic were not the ignorant booby which he exhibits himself, he would have known that the line of flags which he sneers at - extended between Mr. Pugh's store and the Royal Gazette office - embraced Marryatt's code of signals. The yellow flag, particularly noticed, is the letter C of the Admiralty. It was especially appropriate on that occasion, as it is the first letter of the great word - Confederation!

Halifax British Colonist, July 2, 1867

When Artemus Ward lay in his death-bed at Southampton, he turned to a friend and murmured: "What have I done that I should die so young? I never was guilty of a burglary, or even committed the minor offence of killing a publisher or even a newspaper man."

Truro Mirror, November 9, 1867

Wood - Those of our subscribers living in the neighborhood of Newmarket who desire to pay their subscriptions in firewood will oblige by attending to it at once, so that we may be able to contract for any balance which may be required for the year's supply. Any subscriber bringing a cord of good hardwood will receive the balance over and above the subscription to the paper in cash.

Newmarket Era, December 30, 1870

We must decline to publish the poetical effusion sent by someone who signs himself "a subscriber." It will take up too much of our time correcting and preparing it for the compositor.

Newcastle Union Advocate, April 6, 1871

Mr. Charles Brown is the only travelling agent employed by us in the interests of the FARMER, and no subscription should be paid to any other person, unless he can produce written authority to act as our agent.

Fredericton Colonial Farmer, February 12, 1872

Owing to some cause or the other, the Pioneer of last week went abroad with several typographical errors. In one place, "obscure" farmers were made to read "obscene" farmers. We will endeavor to be more guarded in the future.

Alberton Pioneer, November 8, 1876

Today we launch the Daily Times on the rough waters of Canadian journalism, trusting that the staunchness of the craft, the labors of the crew, and the favoring winds of public approval and public support will keep her afloat and enable her to render good public service for many years to come.

Moncton Daily Times, August 13, 1877

Our chief editor, having a very severe cold, feels in bad humor and in consequence our readers are requested to humor themselves as best they can if the editorial columns of the Sorel Pilot are filled up with borrowed and purloined second-hand matter.

Sorel Pilot, August 23, 1877

The Stratford papers are just now engaged in a most undignified warfare of abuse and recrimination. The Times is especially liberal in hurling epithets at the Beacon. "Traitor," "coward," "drunken," "thief," "impudent," "harlot," and "silly" are some of the choice tidbits served up in one column of the Times. Such language is a disgrace to journalism.

Brantford Daily Expositor, December 19, 1878

Gentle reader, we don't wish to appear egotistical, but just compare the quality and quantity of reading matter furnished every week by THE INTERNATIONAL with that of other papers in this region. Then consult your best interests and join the throng of people who are weekly coming forward to contribute their mite of two dollars to the support of this paper. By the way, we may as well intimate to you that it is intended in a few weeks to enlarge THE INTERNATIONAL to double its present size. It will then be the largest and cheapest paper between St. Paul and the North Pole.

Emerson International, January 30, 1879

The extensive circulation of the Herald throughout Conception Bay and the various outport districts of the colony render it a most desirable medium for advertising purposes. We would direct the particular attention of businessmen generally to the above mentioned most significant fact.

Carbonear Herald, July 31, 1879

Someone has left a Bible at the [Winnipeg] Free Press office. It is about as much use there as a gallon of whiskey is at a temperance meeting.

Winnipeg Daily Times, February 4, 1881

A Kincardine man wants to bet that he can sleep for a week. All he has to do is hire himself out in a store that does not advertise in a newspaper.

Lucknow Sentinel, August 26, 1881

The cruel and wicked young man of the Alliston Herald recorded recently in his columns how "Sam Green" was "fooled" on April 1. "Sam" denies the little affair and writes us a long article on fools in general and Alliston fools in particular. We haven't space for the letter, "Sam," and we have our own opinion that people in this section don't care a red cent whether "Sam" was fooled or not.

Collingwood Enterprise, April 20, 1882

CHEEKY - The half demented savage who controls the destinies of that puny and insignificant sheet, the Times, published in the far away desert, which for geographical purposes is dignified with the name Orillia, records his opinion of the way our municipal council works as follows: "Collingwood is slowly, but surely emerging from barbarism. At its last Council meeting a by-law was introduced for the abolition of cow bells and to prevent cows running at large. When a sidewalk is to be built in that old foggy town, her council finds it necessary to pass a by-law to that effect. Orillia does things differently from that; she simply instructs her officer with multitudinous titles to see to it, and the work is done."

Collingwood Enterprise, April 27, 1882

Some scamp has stolen Frank Morrow's educated pig. Though we have heard of no recent changes on the Liberal's editorial staff, the pig-headed articles of that sheet may suggest a clue to the whereabouts of the animal.

Portage La Prairie Weekly Tribune, March 7, 1884

The Society for the Prevention of Cruelty to Animals is a good thing in its way, but it has raised fiends in this community, in comparison with whom the spring poet is an angel. We are inundated with communications on the subject of cruelty to animals. We beg gently, softly, and ever so kindly to suggest to these gushing beings that there is such a thing as cruelty to editors. If they don't let up on their confounded effusions - we give them fair warning - we'll publish some of them one of these fine days, and we'll be hanged if we don't also print their names in the bargain. Why in thunder don't they go for the Royal Gazette, the President of the SPCA's paper? What have we done to be thus afflicted?

Fredericton Evening Capital, April 26, 1884

We have to apologize for the late appearance of the NEWS this week. When the editor of a newspaper gets on one side of the river and the newspaper is on the other, with big hills, an ice jam and high water between them, there is liable to be some confusion in the arrangements. This has been our case. The editor unwittingly placed himself beyond the waters of the mighty Belly, and like all editors, was adverse to taking the cold water to get back again. He preferred something stronger. However, pardon us and we shall promise not to let it occur again if we can help it.

Lethbridge News, December 11, 1885

"VERY VIGOROUS VINDICATION!" - The vacillant genius of the [Paris] Star-Transcript makes a vain, though "very vigorous" effort to be funny in an article with this euphonious title which appears in the last issue of that vapid journal. In this vile, vaniloquent vagary, no one can find either sense or humor - it is simply the vaporiferous ventilation of a velutinous and vacuolated intellect in a state of vagissatation. That is all.

Brant Review, April 16, 1886

The Toronto World is the best journal issued in Ontario. Why? Because it is patriotic, outspoken, spicy, and honest. Long may it live.

Brampton Conservator, May 20, 1887

"Anything fresh?" asked the reporter of our local contemporary as he entered the YMCA rooms at noon today. "Yes, that paint you are leaning against," replied Mr. Orr, and the reporter found that he had been besmeared with paint from stem to stern by the partition which is being frescoed.

St. Thomas Daily Times, January 7, 1888

Last week a man stepped up to us and said he would pay

every cent he owed this office, if he lived till Saturday night. We presume the man died and is still walking around to save funeral expenses. Another said he would pay us in a day or two as sure as he was born. Query: Did the man lie or was he never born? Another said he hoped to go to the devil, if he did not pay us in three days. Haven't seen him since, and suppose he has gone, but we trust he has not hoped in vain. Quite a number have said they would see us tomorrow. These have been stricken blind. One man told us six months ago he would pay us as soon as he got some money. The man would not lie, so of course he has not had a cent since.

Moosomin Courier, February 14, 1889

The meanest man has been found. He lives in Warwick and borrows his local paper, and when he gets through reading it, he rents it to his neighbor at a profit, and then abuses the editor because there is nothing in it.

Petrolia Topic, October 24, 1890

It looks as if the reason the Examiner editor has not made up his mind on the Scott Act [local-option prohibition] question is because he has no mind to make up.

Charlottetown Guardian, January 5, 1891

The marriage of a Louisville editor to an heiress suggests that there is one chance, after all, of an editor getting rich.

Richibucto Review, January 15, 1891

A man who was afraid of thunder crawled into a hollow log as a place of safety during a thunder storm. The thunder rolled, and the rain poured down in torrents, and the old log began to swell up until the poor little fellow was wedged in so he could not get out. All his past sins began passing before him. Suddenly he remembered he hadn't paid his newspaper subscription, and he felt so small that he was able to crawl right out of the log.

Coaticook Observer, April 17, 1891

Brother White advertised for a [servant] girl a couple of weeks ago, and on the 27th his wife presented him with a daughter. There's nothing like advertising in the Mail to get what you want.

Brandon Mail, February 6, 1896

The News-Advertiser of Vancouver is a news pirate of the most pronounced type. It steals the news it publishes concerning the interior districts from the up-country press. There is seldom a day passes that the News-Advertiser makes a "herringbone" of the Miner, and it never has the journalistic courtesy to give credit for the news it appropriates.

Rossland Weekly Miner, November 4, 1897

The Toronto Globe is now known throughout British Columbia as "The Enemy of the West."

Rossland Weekly Miner, January 6, 1898

Chapter Eighteen

This & That

An eclectic array of topics received attention in nineteenth-century newspapers. Out of plain curiosity, Victorian Canadians found the exceptional interesting. They delighted in reading about remarkable accomplishments, economic achievements, firsts, and their country's successes abroad. In particular, they were fascinated by the truly bizarre, such as edible restaurant menus and human oddities. On the other hand, our antecedents also enjoyed learning about less extraordinary events and changes in their world, including everything from the settlement of the West to fashion trends. Indeed, it was a little of this and a little of that which spiced up their newspaper columns.

On Thursday night a male child, about six months old, was found on Albro Street, having evidently been abandoned by its mother. A good Samaritan passing that way found the child, took him to his home, and intends to adopt him.

Halifax Novascotian, January 25, 1869

Good pay - The lightning Company, on Lightning Creek, last week took out 205 ounces of gold from a piece of ground measuring 9 feet by 8 2/3. This week they are getting 100 ounces to the set of timbers and expect to have 400 or 500 ounces at the end of the week.

Cariboo Sentinel, May 28, 1870

Who Can Beat It? Mr. Patrick Maher, of Cold Springs, a hardy celt, lately completed the task of chopping, splitting, and piling one hundred cords of wood in the extraordinarily short time of 26 days. When it is considered that Mr. Maher worked entirely alone during this time, and that he could not work more than from 7 to 8 hours each day, this is surely one of the greatest feats in wood chopping ever accomplished - the greatest we have ever heard of.

Cobourg Sentinel, December 17, 1870

Hard Luck - A miner who came down from Omineca in the ship Otter yesterday, just before arriving in the harbor, had the great misfortune to lose overboard all his hard-earned gains of the season - amounting to 33 ounces of gold. His purse dropped out of his trousers' pocket.

Victoria Daily Standard, October 25, 1871

A female lecturer says that the only decent thing about Adam was a rib, and that went to make something better.

Pictou Colonial Standard, August 5, 1873

The value of fish taken in Nova Scotia during the past year is $6,200,000. We are particularly pleased to notice that the catch of salmon during the year was fifty percent in excess of that in 1872. We are glad to find our fishery officers furnishing such good proof of efficiency.

Amherst Gazette, January 30, 1874

A Brazilian lady is creating a sensation in Paris. She has a yellow carriage, and the wheel hubs are of solid gold. The servants connected with the turnout number four - two in the box and two in the rumble. The harness is gold-tipped and the horses are thoroughbreds.

Paris Star, March 24, 1875

The village of Courtright hasn't a shoemaker. Poor soles.

Clinton New Era, March 25, 1875

Nova Scotia is becoming noted for people of enormous growth. The latest wonder in that way has been discovered at "the Point," Pugwash, in the person of Lizzie Foshay, a little girl of 13, who only weighs 239 pounds and is just one inch short of six feet in height. How's that for high?

Alberton Pioneer, October 4, 1876

In Montreal a new 22 pound baby has an 85 pound mother.

Rimouski Star, February 3, 1877

Nearly half a ton of Ontario butter is among the imports of Messrs. Mahoney & Macdonald now on the road. With our millions of acres of the richest grazing land in the world, and a climate that does not require cattle to be housed in winter, the import of this article must soon be discontinued.

Saskatchewan Herald, September 9, 1878

The great objection to smart children is that when they commence having whiskers, they leave off having brains. Boys who are philosophers at six years of age, are generally blockheads at twenty-one. By forcing children, you get so much into their heads that they become cracked in order to hold it.

Chatham [New Brunswick] *Gleaner*, February 15, 1879

Newfoundland annually extracts from cod livers about 1,250,00 gallons of oil valued at $1,000,000.

Carbonear Herald, July 24, 1879

The plenipotentiary extraordinary of the London Free Press says that Sarnia has more feminine beauties than any other place in Ontario.

Sarnia Observer, June 11, 1880

"Lambton Beauty" is the name of a brand of cigars now being manufactured in Sarnia. Hardly possible to have been named after Sarnia's maidens.

Petrolia Topic, November 14, 1890

It is currently reported that Professor Rooney is a boss Physiognomical Hair Dresser, Facial Operator, Cranium Manipulator and Capillary Abridger. He will shave and cut the hair of the summer tourist with ambidextrous facility at his perambulating salon, market square.

St. Andrew's [New Brunswick] *Bay Pilot*, June 2, 1881

Mrs. Burton of Shefford died recently at the advanced age of 107 years. At the time of her death, the living descendants of the deceased numbered 120.

Bedford Times, February 2, 1883

The "Times" says that a man in Peterborough, who has a great capacity for eating eggs, on a wager devoured 3 dozen and 2 raw eggs before his appetite was satisfied.

Campbellford Herald, April 12, 1883

MOUNT ALLISON COLLEGE, Sackville, from its first organization admitted ladies on equal terms to the regular college classes, and Miss Hattie S. Stewart, daughter of the

Rev. Dr. Stewart, graduated B.A. in regular course in 1882 with honors. The young lady, therefore, enjoys the distinction of being the first regular lady college graduate in Canada. Mount Allison College was, we believe, the first Canadian college to throw open its courses of study and degrees to ladies.

Fredericton Evening Capital, April 24, 1884

William Baker, of Stratford, an invalid, has completed a large inlaid sideboard 8 feet in height and 5½ feet in length, which contains 82,259 separate pieces of wood. It took him two years to make it.

Brussels Post, January 2, 1885

Walkerton claims one of the greatest Canadian gormandizers, according to the Herald. It remarks, "Walkerton can boast of at least one man who is possessed of an extensive appetite. Last Wednesday he ate 2 lbs. of bologna and 8 apples for a start. Then he had a hearty supper, followed by no less than 7 lemons, and topped off with 4 glasses of cider and another apple. And the man still lives." Well, we imagine we have a boy in Dutton who can eat all round that man. Of course, we had considerable to do to dispose of our own rations at the Presbyterians' tea-meeting Monday evening, but when we noticed a boy with his mouth and eyes wide open, and about three-quarters of him inside his biggest brother's pants, we knew he had set his trap for large game. He didn't want to be partial with waiters, so he took well-filled plates from all. He first led off with a quarter of a rooster, a ham sandwich, a piece of mince pie, another of jelly cake, a cup of tea, a tart, and a salmon sandwich, then became nicely interested in another cup of tea, another sandwich, berry pie, fruit cake, fowl, sponge cake, cookies, coffee for a change, lemon pie, and then, after adjusting his brother's pants in order to be more comfortable, finished easily with the following in various quantities: three cups of tea, two sandwiches, five tarts, sponge cake, fruit cake, jelly cake, marble cake, white cake, chocolate cake, loaf cake, feather cake, a twister, five kinds of pie, and other things too numerous to mention, all disposed of without reserve. The only bad result was that the boy's mother had to sew new buttons on the pants the next day.

Dutton Enterprise, January 15, 1885

North Stanbridge - As one of our neighbors was returning from Stanbury last Sunday night, he was suddenly startled by a ghostly apparition, which, just ahead of him, seemed to follow a small creek a short distance and suddenly disappeared. Will says he is at a loss to know whether it was his Satanic Majesty fishing by moonlight or what.

Missisquoi Record, June 12, 1885

A young lady, in a somnambulistic tour a few nights ago, aroused the family of a prominent citizen by rapping at the door at 2 a.m. She was in undressed costume, but wore a blanket. When the gentleman of the house came to the door, she awoke and made herself scarce in a hurry.

Portage La Prairie Weekly Review, November 27, 1885

The past few days have been unusually fine, and the great display of handsome baby carriages and their no less interesting inmates is remarkable, which leads us to believe that there is evidently rivalry in this line.

King's County Weekly Record, September 16, 1887

The old time prejudice against the wearing of wigs and toupees is rapidly dying out. The cause of this is that the improvements made in their manufacture give them a most natural appearance, and the wearer now feels more confident that his wig or toupee cannot be detected so readily as formerly. This change (in Canada) is mostly attributed to Prof. Dorenwend, of Toronto, who makes this line a specialty and invites gentlemen to call him at the Hicks House Hotel on Tuesday and Wednesday, 26th and 27th, and see his samples.

Perth Courier, June 15, 1888

A rather rare occurrence took place near Oshawa one day lately. In one family, a birth, marriage and death occurred within three or four hours of each other.

Bowmanville Canadian Statesman, August 22, 1888

Eight hundred fat cattle are now being held in the environs of Calgary for shipment to England. This will make three train loads of the size usually sent out by the C.P.R. It is expected that the first train will be loaded tomorrow.

Calgary Herald, October 11, 1888

Mrs. J. Milner, of Granville Ferry, has pieced together a quilt containing 2,520 pieces, and not 2 pieces alike in it.

Wolfville Acadian & Berwick Times, January 16, 1891

I.G. Baker & Co.'s office has been moved down to the old Baker mess building. The safe was moved yesterday. It weighs about 7,000 pounds, and its removal was no light undertaking.

Macleod Gazette, March 26, 1891

In 1891, Canada had 800,000 milch cows which produced cheese to the value of $9,608,800 and butter to $602,175. It is estimated that the cheese produce of 1892 will foot up to $10,200,000.

Millbrook Reporter, January 26, 1893

A total of 470 [train] carloads of settlers' effects have passed through Winnipeg this spring, 398 coming from Ontario and 72 from the United States.

Saskatchewan Herald, April 28, 1893

Out of 135 prizes awarded at the World's Fair for cheese, no less than 126 have been captured by Canadians. This is surely creditable to the industry in Canada.

Port Elgin Times, June 28, 1893

S.R. Brill, of the Teeswater creamery, has received a telegram stating that he has been awarded a medal for butter at the World's Fair. Medals were only given to those exhibitors who scored 97 points out of a possible 100.

Port Elgin Times, July 26, 1893

Ontario has been awarded 179 medals for her fruit exhibit at the World's Fair for currants, gooseberries and cherries alone.

Port Elgin Times, October 18, 1893

Buffalo bone pickers are busy on the plains gathering the remains of the old settlers [nickname for buffalo] for shipment to Saskatoon. They have been working so industriously since the railway was opened that they have to go on a several days' journey to fill their carts. The bones sell for about a hundred dollars a carload. Several parties in town are organizing to go gathering. Prairie fires will, therefore, soon be in order, as the grass is burned, so that the bones may be seen.

Saskatchewan Herald, July 21, 1893

A fashion note says that plump girls are all the rage again, and the sale of anti-fat remedies is falling off at an alarming rate. Thus, it appears that there is no great gain without some small losses.

Waterloo County Chronicle, January 13, 1894

Monday was All Fools' Day. There should have been a tremendous celebration.

Surrey Times, April 5, 1895

Hampton Notes - Miss Catherine Travis, the talented daughter of station master Travis, distinguished herself at McGill

College and captured the Prince of Wales Gold Medal. This is the second time in the history of the college that the medal has been taken by a lady. Miss Travis also won a twenty dollar gymnasium prize for physical culture, together with other prizes and classing. The young lady is to be congratulated on her brilliant record.

King's County News, May 2, 1895

The Bloomer is being introduced in Guelph. Last night a woman adorned with a pair was observed riding a bicycle.

Guelph Daily Mercury, July 4, 1896

The latest thing in hotel bills of fare is said to be an edible menu card. It is generally made of biscuit, which the guest eats with his cheese.

Berlin Daily Telegraph, January 5, 1898

The wife of a laborer, named Peterman, living at Morebath, near Tiverton, has just presented her husband with their 25th child.

Berlin Daily Telegraph, January 11, 1898

An Arnprior farmer recently leased his farm to a neighbor, and with the farm leased his son's services. This is looked upon as a species of bondage, but fortunately is not heard of very often these days.

Merrickville Star, July 13, 1899

The McDonald Klondike Bonanza Co., Ltd., which is summer sluicing No. 2 above discovery Bonanza, recently struck exceedingly rich dirt on the lower half of the claim. Very coarse gold was found, among it being a nugget worth $460. Saturday, one pan yielded 30 ounces or $450, another one Sunday produced 54 ounces and still another 62 ounces or $930, reckoned at $15 per ounce.

Dawson Daily News, August 19, 1899

Gazetteer of Newspapers

Alberta

(Calgary) Alberta Tribune
Calgary Herald
Calgary Nor'wester
Cardston Record
Edmonton Bulletin

Lethbridge News
Macleod Gazette
Medicine Hat Times
South Edmonton News

British Columbia

(Barkerville) Cariboo Sentinel
Chilliwack Progress
Kamloops Inland Sentinel
New Westminster Mainland Guardian
Nanaimo Free Press
Nelson Miner
Rossland Weekly Miner

Surrey Times
Vancouver Weekly World
Vernon News
Victoria British Colonist
Victoria British Columbian
Victoria Daily Standard

Manitoba

Brandon Mail
Emerson International
Morden Monitor
Portage La Prairie Weekly Review
Portage La Prairie Weekly Tribune

Wawanesa Enterprise
Winnipeg Daily Times
Winnipeg Daily Tribune
Winnipeg Free Press
Winnipeg Nor'wester

New Brunswick

Chatham Gleaner
Fredericton Colonial Farmer
Fredericton Evening Capital
(Hampton) King's County News
Moncton Daily Times
Newcastle Union Advocate
Richibucto Review

Sackville Borderer
St. Andrew's Bay Pilot
St. Croix Courier
St. John Daily News
St. John Daily Sun
(Sussex) King's County Weekly Record
(Woodstock) Carleton Sentinel

Newfoundland

Carbonear Herald
Harbour Grace Standard
St. John's Morning Chronicle
St. John's Newfoundlander

St. John's Public Ledger
Trinity Weekly Record
Twillingate Sun

Nova Scotia

(Acadia Mines) Londonderry Times
Acadia Mines Week's Doings
Amherst Gazette
Amherst Maritime Sentinel
Antigonish Casket
Baddeck Island Reporter
Baddeck Telephone
Bridgewater Weekly Telephone
Caledonia Gold Hunter

Digby Weekly Courier
Guysboro Gazette
Halifax Acadian Recorder
Halifax British Colonist
Halifax Citizen
Halifax Evening Express
Halifax Evening Reporter
Halifax Herald
Halifax Morning Chronicle

Nova Scotia continued

Halifax Novascotian
Unionist & Halifax Journal
Lunenburg Argus
New Glasgow Eastern Chronicle
North Sydney Herald
Pictou Colonial Standard
Port Hawkesbury Bulletin

Sydney Advocate
(Sydney) Cape Breton Advocate
Truro Advertiser
Truro Mirror
Truro Signal
Wolfville Acadian & Berwick Times
Yarmouth Herald

Ontario

Acton Free Press
(Ailsa Craig) North Middlesex Review
Alexandria Glengarrian
Alliston Weekly Herald
Almonte Gazette
Alvinston Free Press
Aylmer Express
Beaverton Express
Belleville Intelligencer
Belleville Weekly Chronicle
Blenheim News
Bolton Enterprise
Bothwell Times
Bowmanville Canadian Statesman
(Bracebridge) Muskoka Herald
Bradford Witness
Brampton Conservator
Brantford Daily Expositor
Brockville Recorder
Brussels Post
Campbellford Herald
Carleton Place Herald
Chatham Tri-Weekly Planet
Chesterville Record
Clinton New Era
Cobourg Sentinel
Collingwood Enterprise
Cornwall Standard
Deseronto Tribune
Durham Chronicle
Dutton Advance
Dutton Enterprise
Embro Courier
Embro Planet
Fergus News-Record
Galt Reformer
(Goderich) Huron Signal
Gravenhurst Banner
Guelph Advertiser
Guelph Daily Mercury
Hagersville Indian
Hamilton Evening Times
Hamilton Spectator

Hastings Star
Huntsville Forester
Ingersoll Chronicle
Jarvis Record
Kenora News
Kemptville Advance
Kingston Daily News
(Kitchener) Berlin Daily Telegraph
Lanark Era
Lindsay Canadian Post
Listowel Banner
London Advertiser
London Free Press
Lucknow Sentinel
(Manitowaning) Manitoulin Expositor
Markham Economist
Meaford Monitor
Merrickville Star
Midland Free Press
Mildmay Gazette
Millbrook Reporter
Milton Canadian Champion
Mitchell Advocate
Mount Forest Representative
Napanee Beaver
Newmarket Era
Niagara News
Norwich Gazette
Orangeville Sun
Orillia Times
Oshawa Vindicator
Ottawa Citizen
Ottawa Free Press
Ottawa Times
Owen Sound Advertiser
(Paris) Brant Review
Paris Star
Parkhill Gazette-Review
Perth Courier
Peterborough Examiner
Peterborough Review
Petrolia Advertiser
Petrolia Topic

Ontario continued

Picton Gazette
Port Colborne Herald
Port Elgin Times
Port Hope Guide
Prescott Telegraph
Renfrew Mercury
St. Catharines Constitutional
St. Catharines Evening Journal
St. Catharines Weekly News
St. Mary's Argus
St. Mary's Journal
St. Thomas Daily Times
St. Thomas Journal
Sarnia Observer
Schomberg Standard
(Seaforth) Huron Expositor
Shelburne Economist
Simcoe British Canadian
Smith's Falls Echo
Stratford Daily Beacon
Stratford Herald
Sudbury Journal
Tara Leader
Thamesville Herald

(Thunder Bay) Fort William Journal
Tilbury Times
Toronto Daily Telegraph
Toronto Evening News
Toronto Leader
Toronto Mail
Toronto Star
Toronto World
Trenton Courier
Uxbridge Journal
(Walkerton) Bruce Herald
Wallaceburg Herald
Wallaceburg Valley Record
Waterford Express
(Waterloo) Waterloo County Chronicle
Watford Advocate
Watford Guide-News
Whitby Chronicle
Windsor Evening Record
Wingham Times
Woodstock Sentinel
Woodstock Weekly Review
Woodville Advocate

Prince Edward Island

Alberton Pioneer
Charlottetown Daily Examiner

Charlottetown Guardian
(Summerside) P.E.I. Farmer

Quebec

Bedford Times
(Bryson) Pontiac News
Buckingham Post
Coaticook Observer
Granby Gazette
Granby Mail
Huntingdon Canadian Gleaner
Knowlton News & Brome City Advocate
Montreal Gazette
Montreal Star

Ormstown New Dominion
Quebec Daily News
Quebec Mercury
Quebec Morning Chronicle
Rimouski Star
Sherbrooke Daily Record
Sherbrooke Gazette
Sorel Pilot
(Stanbridge East) Missisquoi Record
Stanstead Journal

Saskatchewan

(Battleford) Saskatchewan Herald
Moosomin Courier
Moose Jaw Times
Prince Albert Times

Qu'Appelle Progress
Qu'Appelle Vidette
Regina Leader
Regina Standard

Yukon Territory

Dawson Daily News

(Dawson) Yukon Sun